AFFIRMATIVE ACTION

Other Books in the At Issue Series:

AFFIRMATIVE ACTION

David Bender, *Publisher*
Bruno Leone, *Executive Editor*

Scott Barbour, *Managing Editor*
Brenda Stalcup, *Series Editor*

A. E. Sadler, *Book Editor*

AT ISSUE

An Opposing View

Greenhaven Press, I

San Diego, Californ

Library of Congress Cataloging-in-Publication Data

Affirmative action / A. E. Sadler, book editor.
        p.   cm. — (At issue) (Opposing viewpoints series)
    Includes bibliographical references and index.
    ISBN 1-56510-387-4 (lib. : alk. paper) — ISBN 1-56510-386-6
(pbk. : alk. paper)
    1. Affirmative action programs—United States. I. Sadler, A. E.
II. Series. III. Series: Opposing viewpoints series (Unnumbered)
HF5549.5.A34A4   1996
331.13'3'0973—dc20   95-39058
                                                                          CIP

© 1996 by Greenhaven Press, Inc., PO Box 289009,
San Diego, CA 92198-9009

Printed in the U.S.A.

Every effort has been made to trace owners of copyrighted material.

Table of Contents

Introduction

In 1964, Lyndon B. Johnson signed Executive Order 11246, requiring employers to actively seek inclusion of qualified minorities among their pool of applicants when hiring. This act signalled the birth of affirmative action. At the time, unemployment within the African American community was double that experienced by Caucasians, and the legislation attracted little attention. Since then, however, it has become the source of fiery debate.

Broadly defined, affirmative action refers to efforts to increase educational and employment opportunities for minorities and women. More specifically, it applies to various policies and programs designed to increase the number of minorities and women hired by government and industry and admitted into colleges and universities.

Today, arguments persist that affirmative action, contrary to the claims of its supporters, is a quota system that leads to unfair preferences for members of certain groups. Most people think of quotas as numerical requirements: specific and measurable targets for employers and schools in hiring or admitting acceptable levels of minorities and women. While the original language of Executive Order 11246 addresses the diversity of applicants only, and not those ultimately chosen, some people argue that efforts to meet the numerical goal tend to override all other considerations, most particularly, qualifications, in the final selection process. This practice is in effect "reverse discrimination" they contend, citing multiple instances in which a white male applicant with superior qualifications was turned away from a school or job in favor of a minority. "This system erodes the American ideal that anyone who works hard and plays by the rules has an equal chance to achieve his or her goals," asserts U.S. representative Ron Packard. And such discrimination, he and others maintain, fosters divisiveness, resentment, and interracial disharmony. "Affirmative action pits group against group," Packard wrote in an *American Legion Magazine* news editorial.

Others argue against affirmative action because, as they see it, its programs have done their job and therefore it is time to dismantle them. "Affirmative action played a very, very useful role in opening doors to many people who were wrongly locked out of the system," says Joe Gelman, a civil service commissioner for the city of Los Angeles. "But we have reached the point of diminishing returns." According to California governor Pete Wilson, who also opposes continuing affirmative action, "Even the architects of this system . . . never intended that it would last forever."

Some people insist that affirmative action does not work and never has, claiming that its policies have harmed the very individuals they were designed to help. These critics maintain that affirmative action, by rewarding race or gender rather than merit, casts doubt over the successes of its recipients. Furthermore, they argue, it is premised on the idea that certain groups are inferior and therefore incapable of competing successfully if held to the same standards as everyone else—an inherently discriminatory concept. Self-described beneficiaries of affirmative action like Yale law professor Stephen Carter, whose viewpoint is included in this anthology, have taken a stand against affirmative action due in part to reasons such as these. "Our strategy must be to insist . . . on being treated no differently than anybody else," Carter writes. "Only then will we be able to look boorish interviewers and colleagues (and the genuinely racist ones, too) squarely in the eye."

Supporters of affirmative action argue that it does work and that it is largely responsible for whatever gains minorities and women have attained in business and education since it was introduced. The programs' advocates disagree with opponents who blame existing racial tensions on group preference policies. Rather, they argue, such antagonism proves that the discrimination prompting government to involve itself in ensuring economic equality has not gone away. Prominent leader Jesse Jackson, whose viewpoint is included here, calls for a renewed commitment to affirmative action, arguing that a few decades of race-conscious policies is hopelessly inadequate to redress centuries of racist mistreatment. According to Jamin B. Raskin, a law professor and another contributor to this anthology, some progress has been made in "lifting up the African-American community from the disadvantages and disabilities imposed by hundreds of years of slavery, racism, violence, discrimination, bigotry, and ridicule." But, he adds, true equality and justice for all races, ethnicities, and genders remain distant.

Those who favor affirmative action insist that the need for its programs remains high. They cite statistics showing that positions of status in society remain a nearly exclusive bastion of white males, despite advances implemented through affirmative action policies. "Only six-tenths of one percent of senior management positions are held by African Americans, four-tenths of a percent by Hispanic Americans, three-tenths of a percent by Asian Americans," President Clinton announced in a July 1995 press statement. "White males make up 43 percent of our work force but hold 95 percent of these jobs." U.S. senator Carol Moseley-Braun makes a similar argument, claiming that far from creating reverse discrimination, "affirmative action is about fundamental fairness." She contends that its programs provide "a range of activities to support opportunity and diversity in the workplace and in our economy—the reverse of quotas."

Some who have benefited from affirmative action agree with opponents' complaints that the policy has hurt their credibility. Still, these recipients believe that obtaining any credentials, even those considered questionable, would be substantially more difficult in an environment absent of affirmative action programs. "Like most African-Americans, I'd be glad to dump affirmative action," writes author Farai Chideya, "All I ask in return is that our Government find a way to insure equality in the workplace. I'm still waiting."

In the thirty years since the inception of affirmative action, unemployment among African Americans has grown worse—now more than double the rate for Whites. Whether this confirms that affirmative action has been an abysmal failure or underscores the urgent need to extend its programs becomes one of the subjects debated in *At Issue: Affirmative Action*.

1

People of Color Need Affirmative Action

Jesse L. Jackson

Jesse L. Jackson, a prominent civil rights leader, began his political activism in the mid-1960s when he became involved with Martin Luther King Jr. and the Southern Christian Leadership Conference. Since then, he has directed Operation Breadbasket and founded Operation PUSH, both of which are advocacy groups for minorities and the disadvantaged, and he has campaigned twice for the presidency of the United States. In 1984, Jackson founded the National Rainbow Coalition, a social justice organization of which he is currently the president.

People of color and white women have traditionally been locked out of the broader economic opportunities available to white males, and they are once again being scapegoated as the American public faces uncertainties about what the future global market will bring. Capitalizing on these fears, long-time critics of affirmative action are attempting to turn public opinion against the programs by claiming they are ineffective and that they discriminate against white males, neither of which is true. Statistics reveal that white males continue to monopolize high status positions in society, proving that discrimination continues to persist and that affirmative action is warranted. Three decades of this policy are an inadequate reparation for 250 years of slavery and discrimination. Therefore, America's commitment to affirmative action must be renewed.

Editor's Note: Jesse L. Jackson released the following statement to the National Press Club several months prior to the president of the United States' 1995 review of affirmative action. In it, he responds to arguments put forth by a new Republican congressional majority elected in 1994, which proposes abolishing the programs.

There is great tension in our country today. There are economic fears and insecurities that are real and must be corrected. But there are the hostile voices of fear and demagoguery using the tactic of scapegoating, turning American against American, neighbor against neighbor.

"Affirming Affirmative Action," a press release from Rev. Jesse L. Jackson to the National Press Club, March 1, 1995. Reprinted by permission of the National Rainbow Coalition, Washington, D.C.

Scapegoating the disadvantaged

We have a smiling face on our economy—the stock market has hit its all-time high, Wall Street is booming, the top 20% of all Americans are doing very well. But there is beneath that face a nauseous stomach, the underbelly of our economy, that is not as fortunate. Our rank-and-file workers are feeling insecure and with good reason. For the past 20 years, they've been working longer and making less at less stable jobs. America once exported products; we now export jobs and plants.

Workers feel the pain of the globalization of the economy, the impact of competing with cheaper, less secure, more vulnerable workers. When you combine this with the impact of "reinventing" or reducing government, exporting jobs, downsizing corporations, ending the Cold War (there is nobody to fight), closing military bases, plants, and family farms, while increasing the military budget, it is not surprising that we, as a nation, are feeling anxious.

Nike, Reebok, LA Gear, Westinghouse, Smith Corona, and many of our other manufacturing companies have moved offshore. RCA, once symbolized by the dog listening to its master's voice, is an image which no longer applies. Today, the master speaks a language the dog cannot understand.

Those who have been locked out need the law to protect them from the "tyranny of the majority."

In the face of this profound structural crisis in our national economy, we need leadership to provide a clear analysis and constructive solutions to appease our anxieties. Instead, women and people of color are being used as scapegoats and objects of vilification.

While we witness congressional attacks on Aid to Families with Dependent Children, Congress blindly embraces Aid For Dependent Corporations. There is an attack on welfare but tiptoeing around S&L thieves, buccaneer bankers, a trillion and one-half dollar military budget to defend Europe, Japan, and South Korea at a time when they are able to share the burden of their own defense.

Instead of identifying these real problems and finding real solutions, many are perpetrating falsehoods and spreading myths blaming the weakest in our society for the excesses of the few. The new Republican congressional majority is using affirmative action to divide our nation for political gain.

Myth vs. fact

Affirmative Action is under attack. The Republicans want to rip it. The President wants to review it. We must look at America before Affirmative Action and since Affirmative Action. We must look at the remaining gap in wages between men and women, whites and people of color. We must determine its necessity by data, not by anecdotes.

It is a myth that white males are being hurt and discriminated against because of Affirmative Action programs. White males are 33% of the population, but
- 80% of Tenured Professors
- 80% of the U.S. House of Representatives

- 90% of the U.S. Senate
- 92% of the Forbes 400
- 97% of School Superintendents
- 99.9% of Professional Athletic Team Owners; and
- 100% of U.S. Presidents

Since the inception of this nation, white males were given preferential or deferential treatment—for the right to vote, the right to own land, to apply for loans and institutions of higher education. In the late 1800's white males were given a million acres of oil and soil-rich land under the Homestead Act as a bonus to go west and replace Native Americans. As current statistics show, such preferential treatment carries over to 1995.

It is a myth that Affirmative Action creates preferences for women and people of color. After 250 years of slavery, 100 years of apartheid, and 40 years of discrimination—history, of course, is unbroken continuity—we cannot burn the books, we cannot scorch the Earth. This unbroken record of race and sex discrimination has warranted a conservative remedy—Affirmative Action. Those who have been locked out need the law to protect them from the "tyranny of the majority." That is the genius of our Constitution, with its checks and balances and balance of power. We need not be race neutral, but race inclusive. We need not be color and gender blind, but color- and gender-caring. The Good Samaritan was not blind to a damaged man of another race, another religion, and another language; he was caring.

The conservative remedy of affirmative action seeks to repair the effects of past and *present* discrimination. It creates equal opportunities for people who have been historically and currently discriminated against. Affirmative Action does not mean "quotas"—in point of fact, it is *illegal* for employers to prefer *unqualified* applicants over qualified ones. What Affirmative Action mandates is the use of goals and timetables to diversify our workforce and universities.

Affirmative Action . . . has benefitted blacks, browns, Native Americans, Asians, veterans, and the disabled.

It is a myth that Affirmative Action has hurt people of color, women, or the nation. Affirmative Action has benefitted our entire nation. The first beneficiaries are U.S. corporations. We have the strongest, most diversified workforce in the world. We urge the President to convene corporate leaders and let them assume the burden and the obligation to make a statement sharing their experience of the advantages of having a diversified, educated workforce. Affirmative Action has benefitted white women and their families as a result of two-wage earners in their households. It has benefitted blacks, browns, Native Americans, Asians, veterans, and the disabled. It has turned tax consumers into taxpayers and revenue-generators. It has created a new middle class. It has diversified our workforce and has made us a better nation. I literally went to jail to open up building trades unions so that we might become carpenters and brickmasons and glazers and have the right to work with a skill, and earn a livable wage.

Review must be based on data, not myth

As the President pursues his review it must be based on data, not myth. We urge him to convene the Chair of the EEOC [Equal Employment Opportunity Commission], a rather invisible position, the Chair of the Office of Contract Compliance, and indeed the Chair of the U.S. Civil Rights Commission. And let's have a review, not a retreat. A review to renew a commitment to fairness and to complete unfinished business.

The President is calling for a review. When he does his review, he will discover that Department of Labor statistics illustrate clear disparities in the representation of women and people of color in the American workforce as compared to white men.

In the 1994 labor market, while women represented 51.2% of the U.S. adult population, African Americans 12.4%, and Latinos 9.5%.

- 22% of all doctors were women, 4% African American, 5% Latino
- 24% of all lawyers were women, 3% African American, 3% Latino
- 42% of all professors were women, 5% African American, 2% Latino
- 16% of all architects were women, 1% African American, 3% Latino
- 31% of all scientists were women, 3% African American, 1% Latino
- 8% of all engineers were women, 4% African American, 3% Latino

In May 1994, the National Rainbow Coalition [a civil rights organization] released a study of the National Broadcast Corporation (NBC) which highlights a pattern of racial and gender discrimination in hiring practices in its New York division. ABC and CBS do not vary very much. We found:

- Out of 645 employees of the News Division, 354 were white males, 261 were white females (a total of 96%), 8 were black males, 8 black females, 7 Latino females, 1 Latino male, 3 Asian males and 3 Asian females, 0 Native Americans.
- Of the key employee positions, 142 were white males, 121 were white females, 3 black males, 2 black females, 1 Latino male, 1 Latino female, 0 Asians, and 0 Native Americans.
- Out of 386 employees in NBC's East Coast Entertainment Division, 237 were white males, 130 white females, 6 black males, 3 black females, 5 Latino males, 1 Latino female, 4 Asian males, 0 Asian females and 0 Native Americans.

Patterns of present-day discrimination—of being locked out. This is not a gene factor. This is a pattern based upon cultural, race, and sex bias.

Affirmative Action is still needed

We cannot fall prey to the inane notion that discrimination is an evil of the past. It is today a very painful reality. As the figures above demonstrate, representation of women and people of color in the American workforce has improved, but is hardly sufficient. We still have a long way to go. When Affirmative Action was being enforced, gains were made, but during the Reagan-Bush years, many of the gains were lost. One need look no further than the well-documented disparity in pay between white men, women, and people of color:

- In 1975, median income as a *percentage of white men's salaries* was

74% for African American men, 72% for Latino men, 58% for white women, 55% for African American women, and 49% for Latino women.

- At the height of the Reagan-Bush years in 1985, median income for African American men had dropped to 70%, for Latino men to 68%, rose for white women to 63%, and nominally increased to 57% for African American women and 52% for Latino women.
- In 1993, the figures reflect an increase for African American men to 74%, the rate for Latino men fell to 64%, 70% for white women, and 53% for African American women.

When the President reviews college and professional athletics, he will find great disparities in the positions of power between women, people of color, and white men:

- When the Chargers and the Super Bowl champion 49ers met on Super Bowl Sunday in 1994, there were no people of color or women in positions of power. Yet over 60% of those on the field were African Americans. But beyond the playing field, from coaches to athletic directors, to owners, the same situation is evident in NCAA [National Collegiate Athletic Association] athletic programs. We have effectively gone from picking cotton balls to picking basketballs, baseballs, and footballs. Upward mobility is severely limited.

When the President reviews institutions of higher education, he will find an attack on scholarships and, in effect, the globalization of American doctoral degrees according to a NAFEO (National Association For Equal Opportunity) report:

- Today African Americans comprise only 9.9% of the 12 million students enrollment in two- and four-year undergraduate institutions.
- In 1993, of the 6,496 doctorates awarded in physical sciences only 41 (0.6%) were awarded to African Americans, 89 (1.4%) were awarded to Latinos, and 2,818 (43.3%) were awarded to foreign students (whose countries we subsidize).
- Of all of the 39,754 doctorates awarded in 1993, African Americans received 1,106 (2.8%), Latinos received 834 (2.1%), and foreign students received 12,173 (30.6%).

Lest we forget, forms of preferences have traditionally been granted in higher education on non-racial grounds. For example, we have not yet heard the call to deny children of alumnae special consideration in the admissions process.

When the President reviews government contracting practices, he will find empirical proof that when controls are eliminated, we witness a return to pre–Affirmative Action underrepresentation in our economy. Since the *Croson* decision, minority contracting in the city of Richmond, Virginia—a city of about 70% African American—went from 35% to 1% —reverting back to its pre–Affirmative Action levels.

When the President reviews lending practices, he will find that access to capital and credit is denied to women and people of color because lending decisions are so arbitrary and subjective. Unless there is a reinvestment plan with goals, targets and timetables, the traditionally locked out will never gain access to capital. The contract is useless without the capital. Women and minorities have often had to joint venture with larger, white male firms in order to obtain the necessary capital.

A renewed commitment

Upon completion of his review, we urge the President to renew his commitment to Affirmative Action and enforce Affirmative Action laws as a way of expanding our economy and making us bigger and better and stronger. We hope that he will make the Equal Employment Opportunity Commission and the Office of Contract Compliance and Civil Rights Commission visible agencies and forces for good. The falsely accused need protection, and hope, and opportunity, not scapegoating, and review, and divisiveness, and undue blame.

2

Women Need Affirmative Action

Marcia D. Greenberger

Marcia D. Greenberger is founder and copresident of the National Women's Law Center, a Washington, D.C.–based organization that functions as the legal arm of the women's movement.

Women of today need affirmative action as much as ever. Gains made during the last thirty years of its implementation have helped women (mostly white women), yet have fallen short of the goal of full equality throughout American society. Surveys reveal that dramatic gaps remain in income and professional status between men and women. Affirmative action is an effective corrective tool, as demonstrated by the greater inroads made by women in companies that are government contractors and are therefore mandated to adhere to its goals.

Editor's note: The following viewpoint was given as testimony on May 2, 1995, before the U.S. House of Representatives Committee on Economic and Educational Opportunities' Subcommittee on Employer-Employee Relations.

A ffirmative action programs have played a critical role in opening up opportunities for women and minorities to begin to take their rightful place in our society, and these measures are as urgently needed today as ever.

Barriers for women remain pervasive

Discrimination against women is deeply rooted in our society. For the first 150 years of the Republic, American women lacked the most fundamental right of citizenship—the right to vote. Throughout most of our history, laws that barred women from engaging in certain occupations, from the practice of law to bartending, were upheld. Many of the nation's premier colleges and universities were once completely closed to women. Not long ago, the "want ads" listed openings for women and for men separately, and

Marcia D. Greenberger, testimony given before the U.S. House of Representatives Committee on Economic and Educational Opportunities, Subcommittee on Employer-Employee Relations, May 2, 1995.

some employers told women (but not men) with young children they need not apply at all. Sex discrimination in employment has been prohibited by federal law only since enactment of the Civil Rights Act of 1964, and in education only since the Education Amendments of 1972.

The notion that women lag behind because they want to . . . is simplistic and demonstrably wrong.

While much has changed in recent years, women are still second class citizens in many ways. For example:

• According to the March 1995 report of the Glass Ceiling Commission, 95 to 97% of the senior managers of Fortune 1000 industrial and Fortune 500 companies are male. In the Fortune 2000 industrial and service companies, only 5% of senior managers are women (and virtually all of these are white).[1]

• An earnings gap exists between women and men across a wide spectrum of occupations. In 1991, for example, women physicians earned 53.9% of the wages of male physicians, and women in sales occupations earned only 59.5% of the wages of men in equivalent positions.[2] In 1993 women still earned, on average, only 71.5 cents for every dollar earned by men.[3]

• While women are over half the adult population[4] and nearly half the workforce in this country,[5] women remain disproportionately clustered in traditionally female jobs with lower pay and fewer benefits.[6] For example, in 1991 one in four working women worked in an administrative support job,[7] and 82% of administrative workers in all industries are women.[8]

• While the gender gap in higher education has narrowed, and women now earn roughly half of all bachelor's and masters degrees, they still lag behind in many respects. Women earn only about one-third of doctorate and first professional degrees, and remain underrepresented in many areas not traditionally studied by women. In 1992, women received only about 8.5% of undergraduate engineering degrees, *no* doctorate degrees in engineering, and less than 22% of doctorate degrees in mathematics and the physical sciences.[9]

• Women remain severely underrepresented in most non-traditional professional occupations as well as blue collar trades. For example, women are only 8.6% of all engineers; 3.9% of airplane pilots and navigators; less than 1% of carpenters; 18.6% of architects; and just over 20% of doctors and lawyers. Women are over 99.3% of dental hygienists, but are only 10.5% of dentists.[10]

• 65% of the 62 million working women in the United States earn less than $20,000 annually, and 38% earn less than $10,000.[11]

• Even where women have moved into occupations and professions in significant numbers, they have not moved *up* to the same degree. Women are 23% of lawyers,[12] but only 1 1 % of partners in law firms.[13] Women are 48% of all journalists, but hold only 6% of the top jobs in journalism.[14] Women are 72% of elementary school teachers, but only 29% of school principals.[15]

• Minority women have lagged particularly far behind in both employment and education. In 1993, for example, Black women earned a median income of $19,816, compared to $22,023 for white women and $31,089 for white men. Hispanic women earned a median income of $16,758.[16] Even in sectors where women have made inroads into management, minority women continue to be underrepresented. In the banking industry, only 2.6% of executive, managerial and administrative jobs were held by Black women, and 5% by Hispanic women, compared to 37.6% by white women. In the hospital industry, Black and Hispanic women each held 4.6% of these jobs, while white women held 50.2%.[17] Minority women also earn fewer college degrees than white women. In 1992, white women made up 42.3% of college undergraduates and 48.1% of graduate students; minority women were only 13.4% of undergraduates and 8.4% of graduate students.[18]

• Although white men constitute a minority of both the total workforce (47%)[19] and of college educated persons (48%)[20], they dominate the top jobs in virtually every field.[21] Moreover, white males' median weekly earnings in 1993 were 33% higher than those of any other group in America.[22] The earnings of non-Hispanic white men were 49% higher than those of any other group.[23]

How can these disparities be explained? The evidence is overwhelming that they are the result, in large measure, of discrimination. Sex discrimination, including sexual harassment, continues to be a fact of life in our society. In 1993, 11,908 sex discrimination and sexual harassment charges were filed with the EEOC [Equal Employment Opportunity Commission].[24] That number rose to 14,420 in 1994.[25]

In a 1994 survey by the U.S. Labor Department, 61% of women surveyed said they had little or no likelihood of advancement; and 14% of white women and 26% of minority women reported losing a job or promotion because of sex or race.[26] The Glass Ceiling Commission report cites another study finding that 25% of the women surveyed felt that "being a woman/sexism" was the biggest obstacle they had to overcome, and 59% said they had personally experienced sexual harassment on the job.[27]

These women have made the same career choices as men, worked the same hours as men, yet still earn less.

The notion that women lag behind because they want to—that is, because they would rather work less, or in lower-paying jobs, or not at all— is simplistic and demonstrably wrong. While some women clearly choose to devote themselves to family concerns or to jobs with lower pay for a range of reasons, such choices simply do not explain the disparities. A study cited in the Glass Ceiling Commission report found, for example, that women in senior management worked the same number of hours per week as their male counterparts.[28] Another study, just reported, shows that after about 11 years on medical school faculties, 23% of men but only 5% of women had achieved the rank of full professor—and the gap persisted when the researchers held constant the numbers of hours worked per week.[29] These women have made the same career choices as men, worked the same hours as men, yet still earn less. Discrimination is clearly still with us.

What is affirmative action for women?

As we engage in this debate, it is important to be clear about what affirmative action is—and what it is not.

In employment, examples of affirmative action programs are recruitment and outreach efforts to include qualified women in the talent pool when hiring decisions are made, training programs to give all employees a fair chance at promotions, and in some cases the use of flexible goals and timetables (not quotas) as benchmarks by which to measure progress toward eliminating severe underrepresentation of qualified women in specific job categories.

In education, affirmative action programs for women include grants and graduate fellowship programs aimed at helping women move into fields where their participation has been discouraged, such as engineering, math and the physical sciences. They also include outreach and education programs to ensure the participation of women in apprenticeship training in the skilled trades.

For women business owners, affirmative action programs include laws that encourage or require government agencies and contractors to do business with qualified women-owned companies, as well as programs providing financial, management and technical assistance to women business owners.

Affirmative action is not quotas

Affirmative action is not "quotas" or the substitution of numerical dictates for merit-based decisions. Some affirmative action plans include the management tools of numerical goals or targets for representation of women or minorities, and timetables for meeting those objectives. But the courts have held that these goals and timetables must be flexible and take into account such factors as the availability of *qualified* candidates. They may not constitute "blind hiring by the numbers"; if they do, they are unlawful.

The program that imposes affirmative action requirements on federal contractors, under Executive Order No. 11246, expressly states that "goals may not be rigid and inflexible quotas which must be met, but must be targets reasonably attainable by means of applying every good faith effort to make all aspects of the entire affirmative action program work."[30]

Johnson v. Transportation Agency of Santa Clara County, illustrates the use of flexible goals in practice. There were no women in the agency's 238 "skilled craft worker" positions, which included road dispatchers. Under its affirmative action plan, the agency set a target for increased employment of women in this category (and others in which they had been underrepresented), and in its effort to meet the goal it took gender into account in deciding to promote a woman, rather than a man with substantially equal qualifications, to road dispatcher. Gender was only one factor among many considered, and the woman who received the promotion was fully qualified for the job. The Supreme Court ruled that this constituted a reasonable approach to eliminating an obvious gender imbalance in the workforce.

Affirmative action works

Affirmative action programs make a difference. The reason they work is that they are an effective way to neutralize the biases, stereotypes and prejudices that often seep into selection processes, consciously or unconsciously. Supervisors making hiring or promotion decisions rarely engage in the purely objective, scientific exercise that is sometimes imagined. They are human beings making subjective judgment calls, and their subjective judgment is inevitably influenced by the natural tendency we all have to feel most comfortable with people like ourselves. But affirmative action programs force employers to reach out beyond the "old boys network" to which they would naturally gravitate, and to give fair consideration to candidates who are qualified but who don't fit their preconceptions. Without affirmative action, the woman in the *Johnson* case, who became her agency's first woman road dispatcher ever, undoubtedly would have been passed over by the men who interviewed her because they didn't think a woman could do the job.

Thus, affirmative action programs are slowly making an impact. A government study showed that women made greater gains in employment at companies doing business with the federal government, and therefore subject to federal affirmative action requirements, than at other companies: female employment rose 15.2% at federal contractors, and only 2.2% elsewhere. The same study showed that federal contractors employed women at higher levels and in better paying jobs than other firms.[31]

Equal opportunity for women is still a long way off.

Many individual companies that have adopted affirmative action plans have demonstrated the impact on women. For example, after IBM set up its affirmative action program, its number of female officials and managers more than tripled in less than ten years.[32]

Affirmative action requirements have changed entire industries. In 1978, the Labor Department's Office of Federal Contract Compliance Programs (OFCCP) reviewed the employment practices of the five largest banks in Cleveland. Three years later, the percentage of women officials and managers at these institutions had risen more than 20%. When OFCCP first looked at the coal mining industry in 1973, there were no women coal miners. By 1980, 8.7% were women.[33] Litigation against police and fire departments and the construction trades has resulted in affirmative action plans that have produced dramatic increases in the employment of women (and minorities) in those fields as well.[34] In 1983, for example, women made up 9.4% of the nation's police, and 1.0% of firefighters. By 1993, women were 16% of police, and 3.7% of firefighters.[35]

Women-owned businesses, which have also benefited from affirmative action, have increased since 1982 by more than 57%. Today there are some 7.7 million women-owned businesses, employing more people than all of the Fortune 500 companies combined.[36]

Affirmative action benefits everyone

In addition, programs that increase opportunities for women and minorities are beneficial to our whole society in numerous ways:

• Affirmative action programs that help women advance in the workplace are helping their families to make ends meet. Most women, like men, work because of economic need; indeed, many women are the sole source of support for their families.[37]

• Replacing the "old boys network" with job postings, outreach and training ensures that all workers—women and minorities, but white males, too—have a fair shot at advancing in the workplace.

• Affirmative action programs expand the talent pool for businesses to draw on, and many companies report that a diverse workforce has led to enhanced performance and productivity. DuPont Co. set—and exceeded—higher goals than any affirmative action regulations required, and the company reports that it has been rewarded by the development of new ideas and markets.[38]

• Diversity in our colleges and universities improves the learning process for everyone. As Justice Lewis Powell wrote in the *Bakke* case, "the 'nation's future depends upon leaders trained through wide exposure' to the ideas and mores of students as diverse as this Nation of many peoples."[39]

• Enrollment and scholarship programs that promote diversity in professional schools indirectly serve the public in dramatic ways. For example, it is surely no accident that the advancement of women in fields of medical science has been accompanied by increased attention to women's health issues such as breast cancer and expanded research in those areas.

• Communities benefit from affirmative action in myriad other ways. For example, increased recruitment and training of women police officers, prosecutors, judges and court personnel has led to an improvement in the handling of domestic violence cases and the treatment of domestic violence like the crime that it is—which benefits women, children and all other members of the family and the community who are affected by violence in the home.

Conclusion

Recruitment, outreach, training and other affirmative action programs have opened doors for women in the workplace, in our nation's learning institutions, and in other areas of our society. But equal opportunity for women is still a long way off. Eliminating or curtailing affirmative action would not only halt the forward progress that women, as well as minorities, have been able to achieve; it would mark a giant leap backward in this nation's journey toward equal opportunity for all.

References

1.   Federal Glass Ceiling Commission [FGCC], *Good For Business: Making Full Use of the Nation's Human Capital*, iii-iv (1995).

2.   U.S. Department of Labor, Women's Bureau, *Women Workers: Trends and Issues* 35 (1993).

3.   National Committee on Pay Equity, "The Wage Gap: 1993," citing U.S. Dept. of Commerce, Census Bureau, "Current Population Reports," Series P-60.

4.   U.S. Dept. of Commerce, Census Bureau, *Statistical Abstract of the United States* 13 (1994).

5.   *Id.* at 396. *See also*, U.S. Dept. of Labor, Women's Bureau, "Working Women Count!" at 10 (1994).

6. Employee Benefits Research Institute, Sources of Health and Characteristics of the Uninsured, Analysis of the March 1993 Current Population Survey, Issue Brief No. 145, at 61 (Jan. 1994) (women are heavily concentrated in jobs paying under $20,000 where 82% of the uninsured workers are also located).

7. 9 to 5, "Profile of Working Women," at 1 (1992-93 edition) (data compiled from United States Bureau of Labor and Census Bureau statistics).

8. Equal Employment Opportunity Commission [EEOC], *Job Patterns for Minorities and Women in Private Industry*, table 1, at 1-36 (1993).

9. U.S. Department of Education, National Center for Education Statistics, "Digest of Education Statistics," table 239 (1994).

10. U.S. Dept. of Commerce, *supra* note 4, at 407-409.

11. U.S. Bureau of the Census, Current Population Reports, "Money Income of Households, Families, and Persons in the United States: 1992," Series P-60, No. 184, Table 31.

12. U.S. Dept. of Commerce, *supra* note 4, at 407.

13. Curan and Carson, American Bar Foundation, "The Lawyer Statistical Report" (1994).

14. "A Long Way To Go," *Newsweek*, April 24, 1989, at 74.

15. Commission on Professionals in Science and Technology, *Professional Women and Minorities: A Total Human Resource Data Compendium* 142, Table 5-11 (1994).

16. Institute for Women's Policy and Research, "The Wage Gap: Woman's and Men's Earnings," (1995) (citing unpublished data of the U.S. Bureau of the Census, Current Population Reports).

17. FGCC, *supra* note 1, at 79.

18. U.S. Department of Education, *supra* note 9, at table 203.

19. Cheryl Russell & Margaret Ambry, *American Incomes* 155, 158, 163 *citing*, Bureau of the Census Current Population Reports, "Money Income of Households, Families, and Persons in the United States: 1991," Series P-60, No. 180 (in 1991, 133,836,000 people over age 15 worked; 62,477,000, or 47%, of these were white men).

20. U.S. Bureau of the Census, Current Population Reports, "Poverty in the United States: 1991, "Series P-60, No. 181, table 11 (of the 34,025,000 people aged 25 or older who completed college, 16,578,000, or 48%, were white males).

21. FGCC, *supra* note 1, at iii-iv. *See also*, EEOC, *supra* note 8 (showing that women managers are severely underrepresented in, among many other industries, the mining, construction, banking, hospital, and women's clothing industries).

22. U.S. Dept. of Commerce, *supra* note 4 at 429.

23. *Id.* (computed from Bureau of Labor Statistics, "Employment and Earnings," Jan. 1995, at 207).

24. Unpublished computerized data compiled by EEOC field offices.

25. *Id.*

26. U.S. Dept. of Labor, Women's Bureau, *supra* note 5, at 7.

27. FGCC, *supra* note 1, at 148.

28. FGCC, *supra* note 1, at 151.

29. Leslie Miller, "Women trail men in med school tenure," *USA Today*, April 13, 1995.

30. 41 C.F.R. § 60-2.12(e).

31. Citizen's Commission on Civil Rights, *Affirmative Action to Open the Doors of Job Opportunity*, 123-129 (1984).

32. *Id.*

33. *Id.*

34. *Id.*

35. U.S. Dept. of Commerce, *supra* note 4, at 409.

36. National Foundation for Women Business Owners, "Research Highlights" (1995).

37. Department of Labor, Women's Bureau, *supra* note 2, at 11.

38. Jonathan Glater & Martha Hamilton, "Affirmative Action's Corporate Converts," *Washington Post*, March 19, 1995, at H1.

39. *Regents of University of California v. Bakke*, 438 U.S. 265, 313 (1978) (quoting *Keyishian v. Board of Regents*, 385 U.S. 589, 603 (1967)).

3

Society Needs Affirmative Action to Fight Discrimination

Jamin B. Raskin

Jamin B. Raskin is a professor of law and assistant dean at American University's Washington College of Law. He served on the Clinton-Gore Transition Team's Justice Department/Civil Rights cluster and as Washington-area board member and general counsel for the National Rainbow Coalition. Coauthor of The PC Indictment, *Raskin has written extensively on civil rights and racial issues.*

Today's opponents of affirmative action decry its practice of gender and minority group preferences and call for a return to the "color-blind" and merit-based policies of the past. Yet such policies never existed: America's history is marked by racism and discrimination. Even the term "color-blind" originated as part of a Supreme Court justice's vision of de facto white supremacy prevailing in the aftermath of the Civil War. "Merit" inherently mirrors the cultural values of those who define it. Hence, America's social and economic institutions, which are controlled almost exclusively by white males, require the external guidelines of affirmative action to recognize and reward the merit of minorities and women.

After Reconstruction ended, there were four principal mechanisms for restoring white supremacy in the 1800s. The first was the use of pseudo-scientific explanations of black inferiority—such as phrenology, the study of brain sizes—to justify social and economic inequality. The second was the systematic undermining of black political power through disenfranchisement schemes such as literacy tests, grandfather clauses and poll taxes, as well as violent intimidation. The third was the use by states of the criminal justice system to criminalize, incarcerate, subordinate and terrorize the black community. The fourth mechanism, which began almost immedi-

Jamin B. Raskin, "Affirmative Action and Racial Reaction," *Z Magazine*, May 1995. Reprinted with permission.

ately with Reconstruction itself in the 1870s, was an ideological and political assault on any use of race-conscious government policies or programs to uplift the social or economic position of the black community.

The real political energy behind the anti-PC [political correctness] campaign has always come from boiling white resentment over affirmative action.

The parallels today are haunting. *The Bell Curve*, the best-selling pseudoscientific diatribe by Charles Murray and Richard Herrnstein, has revived the legitimacy of theories about the genetic mental inferiority of African-Americans and other racial minorities. Profound differences among the races in wealth, income, power and position are now enthusiastically defended with two letters: IQ. The conservative journal *Society* publishes an article by racist Philip Rushton linking crime rates to genetic racial differences. Meanwhile, with the 1993 case *Shaw v. Reno*, the most outrageous judicial decision in at least two decades, the Supreme Court threatens to cut in half the number of African-Americans in Congress. In *Shaw*, the Court essentially proclaimed a new presumptive constitutional right—under the Equal Protection clause!—for whites to be in the majority in congressional and state legislative districts, a right that can only be overcome if an African-American majority is in a neatly drawn and "compact" district. This judicial attack nicely mirrors the growing marginalization of black interests in the Democratic and Republican Parties. Furthermore, the War on Drugs, combined with the unleashing of primitive impulses in the public and the TV-fed mania for more prisons, has led to a wholesale criminalization of the African-American community. The rate of incarceration among blacks is seven times that of the national average. On any given day in the big cities like Baltimore and Washington, DC, four out of every ten African-American men between the ages of 18 and 45 are in prison, in jail, on probation, on parole, or awaiting trial.

Finally, the ferocious and mounting public assault on affirmative action promises to undo any race-conscious efforts by the government to uplift the besieged black population. And so white supremacy is being restored, and the second Reconstruction—the modern Civil Rights movement—fast unraveled.

The campaign against affirmative action

The assault on affirmative action is the logical culmination of the popular campaign against "political correctness," which began in the late 1980s. The enemies of the thing called "PC" have enjoyed kicking around multiculturalism and deconstruction the last several years, but the real political energy behind the anti-PC campaign has always come from boiling white resentment over affirmative action. Now it is likely that the days are numbered for this exceedingly modest program to desegregate American life.

The Republican Party, which knows a wedge issue when it sees one, has decided to ride white resentment all the way to the White House by making affirmative action the Willie Horton of 1996. The crucial arena is the "California Civil Rights Initiative," a proposed 1996 ballot measure that would ban "preferential treatment" of racial minorities by the state of California, including municipalities and universities. In this state with more presidential electoral college votes than any other, Republicans are eager to shatter the 1996 electorate along racial and ethnic lines.

The hysteria over affirmative action proceeds in the face of massive evidence of continuing white male dominance in society.

The brainchild of two white academics who seem to blame affirmative action for everything that has ever gone wrong in their lives, the California measure is spreading like political wildfire. As both Republicans and Democrats in other states rush to take up similar proposals, Republican Senators and presidential hopefuls Phil Gramm and Bob Dole are moving to purge the federal government of all affirmative action. President Clinton, standing firm against the right—as was to be expected from his steadfast loyal support for Lani Guinier [candidate for assistant attorney general whose nomination was withdrawn amid pressure from conservatives] and Joycelyn Elders [asked to resign as U.S. surgeon general after publicly advocating the inclusion of information about masturbation in sex education programs], clears his throat and says that he wants to "reconsider" and "review" the various affirmative action programs and get rid of the ones that are not fair.

The hysteria over affirmative action proceeds in the face of massive evidence of continuing white male dominance in society. The Glass Ceiling Commission, created by Elizabeth Dole when she was Secretary of Labor in the Bush administration, recently found that white men occupy 97 percent of senior management positions in Fortune 1000 and Fortune 500 corporations. African-Americans are found in about one-half of one percent of these top jobs, and there are even fewer Hispanics and Asian-Americans. In the private sector generally, African-Americans have just 2.5 percent of executive positions and black men who have professional degrees still earn less than four-fifths of the salaries earned by their white equivalents. Black women, facing double bias, earn three-fifths the amount that white men earn. Of course, African-Americans and other minorities, as well as women generally, form a greater presence in the public sector (one reason the public sector is in danger), but the ranks of top leadership are still almost all-white. There are no African-American governors in the United States, and out of 100 U.S. Senators, Carol Mosely Braun of Illinois is the only African-American.

Anti–affirmative action rhetoric: an historical echo

The complaint against affirmative action today boils down to the idea that "statist" university and government bureaucrats are compromising "traditional" and "historic" notions of "objective merit," "color-blindness" and "neutrality" by showing "preferential treatment" toward "unqualified" racial minorities and women. This "reverse discrimination" causes "unfairness" to that most victimized social group, white men, and, perhaps worst of all, "stigmatizes" its intended beneficiaries—minorities themselves.

These complaints form an historical echo of the rhetoric used to assail federal efforts to uplift the black community during the Reconstruction period following the Civil War. Opposition to Reconstruction, as described by Eric Foner in his brilliant study, came not merely from unrepentant Confederates and racists but Republican white liberals in the north who quickly tired of the whole project of fighting racism, found social change difficult and expensive, despised all "class legislation," and wanted to move on to "the 'living issues' of the Gilded Age."

Throughout its short history, Reconstruction involved aggressive race-conscious efforts to improve the lives and communities of the freedmen. These efforts became a lightning rod for criticism: they were said to be fat state subsidies that unfairly penalized innocent whites and taught blacks self-destructive habits of indolence and dependence. The low-brow version of such criticism is nicely captured in a piece of cartoon-style campaign literature published by the Democratic Party in Pennsylvania in 1866, just one year after the Civil War ended, when Southern whites were busy replacing slavery with a system of closely controlled labor exploitation and white violence against blacks was still pervasive.

The Democratic broadside cartoon, reprinted in Foner's *Reconstruction*, pictures a purportedly lazy black man with exaggerated features resting in the shade while a white man sweats himself chopping wood. The text reads: "The Freedmen's Bureau! An Agency To Keep the *Negro* in Idleness at the *Expense* of the White Man." Above the cartoon figure of the black man it reads: "Freedman's Bureau! Negro Estimate of Freedom! Freedom and No Work. Uncle Sam Will Have to Keep Me." And then in putative black dialect the caption reads: "Whar is de use for me to work as long as dey make dese appropriations." The caption near the white figure reads: "The White Man Must Work to Keep His Children and Pay His Taxes."

The more genteel critics of Reconstruction dressed up the project of racial reaction in the modern language of objectivity and meritocracy.

But the more genteel critics of Reconstruction dressed up the project of racial reaction in the modern language of objectivity and meritocracy. Republican reformers at the time believed in a science of society based on the laws of classical liberalism—"free trade, the law of supply and demand, and the gold standard." To them, "the economic and social policies of Reconstruction governments" were "unacceptable examples of 'class legislation,'" and Reconstruction "increasingly seemed to exemplify all the deleterious consequences of state activism." They argued that "the nation had done all it could for blacks; it was up to the freedmen to make their own way in the world." In 1867 the liberal *Nation* asserted: "The removal of white prejudice against the Negro depends almost entirely on the Negro himself." Public legislation could not relieve the "great burden" weighing down on the African race: its "want of all the ordinary claims to social respectability." By 1871, even Senator Carl Schurz, who had been a prominent anti-slavery agitator before the Civil War, was now maintaining that the rights and fortunes of blacks could not be secured by government. He told the Senate: "There are many social disorders which it is very difficult to cure by laws. "

When we turn to the real world, we find not centuries of color-blindness and objective merit but centuries of racism, slavery and discrimination.

Such rhetoric rankled blacks. For "behind reformers' clamor against 'class legislation' and admonitions to the freedmen to 'work out their own destiny,' they discerned a refusal to acknowledge blacks' unique historical experience, and a cruel indifference to their fate." The radical William Whipper told Liberals opposing the Freedman's Bureau and other special efforts on behalf of the former slaves that "the white race have had the benefit of class legislation ever since the foundation of our government."

One issue separating the Reconstruction radicals from liberal reformers was the proposal for a civil service system. White liberals at the time favored the idea of civil service because they thought it would permit the most enlightened and cultured men to govern. Public servants with a scientific outlook would replace the irrational operations of the big-city ethnic machines in the North and the dangerous excesses of congressional Reconstruction in the South. But, as Foner points out, blacks readily perceived "that civil service reform would effectively bar 'the whole colored population' from office."

Blacks saw that the suddenly emerging conception of job merit, wholly ahistorical and abstracted from circumstance, clashed with the historical imperative of racial justice and inclusion.

Anti–affirmative action rhetoric

Like the arguments directed against Reconstruction, today's critiques of affirmative action come dressed up in different styles of political rhetoric. Consider two poles. At the high end of emotional honesty but low end of intellectual respectability, we find material which, like the 1866 Pennsylvania Democratic cartoon flyer, mixes grotesque racist caricature of African-American language and intelligence with freewheeling factual distortion about the effects of affirmative action. A splendid and paradigmatic success in this genre was the early-80's *Dartmouth Review*'s feature story on affirmative action written in what was supposedly a parody of black speech. The article, entitled *Yo, Man, This Sho' Ain't No Jive* included sentences like: "Now we be comin' to Darmut and be up over our 'fros in studies, but we still be not graduatin' Phi Beta Kappa."

At the other pole—the high end of intellectual respectability but the low end of emotional honesty—we find critiques which eschew racial caricature but profess nostalgia for color-blind meritocracy and deep racial sympathy for African-Americans and other minorities harmed by the stigma of affirmative action. A seminal example of this genre was Dinesh D'Souza's much-celebrated book *Illiberal Education*, which concluded that, with affirmative action and its associated symptoms, the university now teaches "that standards and values are arbitrary," "that individual rights are a red flag signaling social privilege, and should be subordinated to the claims of group interest," "that double standards are acceptable as long as they are enforced to the benefit of minority victims," and "that a multiracial society cannot be based on fair rules that apply to every person but must rather be held together with a forced rationing of power among separatist groups." In this forlorn world of meritocracy lost, D'Souza's most passionate concern is for "the young blacks, Hispanics and other certified minority-group members in whose name the victims' revolution is being conducted," for they "are the ones worst served by the American University's abandonment of liberal ideals."

Before parsing the various arguments contained here, it is at least illuminating, if not necessarily decisive on the merits, to note that the *Dartmouth Review* article ridiculing affirmative action in putatively "black speech" was published under the stewardship of its founding editor, who was none other than Dinesh D'Souza himself. Later, after serving as a domestic policy aide in the Reagan White House, he became a fellow at the American Enterprise Institute and wrote, in much softer tones, the book quoted in the second passage, arguing that affirmative action should be jettisoned because it stigmatizes minorities and makes them think of themselves as victims.

One does wonder at what point D'Souza started worrying about the stigmatization of minorities. His defiant editorship of the *Dartmouth Review* also produced an interview with a former KKK chieftain (which was adorned with a staged photograph of an African-American man swinging by neck from a tree on the Dartmouth campus), prominent display of the quaint aphorism—"The only good Indian is a dead Indian," and the publication—against their express wishes—of the names of members of the Gay Student Alliance. Perhaps D'Souza is telling us that he was driven to such vicious extremes because affirmative action creates "a malignance that spreads through university life"—and he caught it. The alternative explanation is that he brought the malignance to campus with him, spread it around, used it on his job application to the Reagan White House and American Enterprise Institute, and now repackages it as a reasonable man's love of merit and Western tradition.

The rhetoric of legal color-blindness flowed directly out of the conviction that whites could maintain their absolute dominance in society.

But D'Souza is not alone in trading in primitive racist invective for the magisterial tones of a wise man defending grand institutions against "politicized" erosion from within. Take the comically unself-conscious James J. Kilpatrick, Virginia gentleman-poseur who writes: "I worry about racial tensions, and I worry that all the posturing gestures of 'diversity' and 'multiculturalism' and 'affirmative action' are making bad matters worse.

Our country ideally should be colorblind. We have become color obsessed."
These somber professions of faith in color-blindness from Kilpatrick would
be easier to stomach had he not been the leading champion of "massive re-
sistance" to school desegregation in Virginia in the 1950s. In those days, his
pen dripped with color-obsessed poison like: "in terms of values that last,
and mean something, and excite universal admiration and respect, what
has man gained from the history of the Negro race? The answer, alas, is 'virtually nothing.' From the dawn of civilization to the middle of the twenti-
eth century, the Negro race, as a race, has contributed no more than a few
grains of sand to the enduring monuments of mankind."

Indeed, as Garrett Epps has pointed out, Kilpatrick's "standard rhetorical strategy" in denouncing civil rights protections today is to state in
melancholy terms that he has "until now been a firm supporter of civil
rights measures, but that this decision or bill finally goes too far." For example, in a December 7, 1988 attack on a Supreme Court decision finding
that the Voting Rights Act applies to the election of judges, Kilpatrick wrote
that: "I ardently supported [the Voting Rights Act of 1965] because I knew,
as only a white Southerner can know, what chicanery my people had employed to prevent blacks from voting." But in an April 20, 1965 article entitled "Must We Repeal the Constitution to Give the Negro the Vote?" Kilpatrick made his feelings about the Voting Rights Act unmistakably clear.
The proposed act, he argued, "strikes with the brute and clumsy force of a
wrecking ball at the very foundations of American federalism."

The political "transformation" of these conservative writers is in-
structive because it teaches us that the lofty rhetoric of neutrality and
merit has a very short history indeed. In the case of many detractors of
affirmative action, the discovery of meritocratic ideology was preceded by
a much longer and more authentic period of unabashed racial hostility.
Could it be that the enemies of the black community are finding themselves more effective posing as its friends?

Color-blindness and history

But let us take D'Souza and Kilpatrick and friends at their present word
and suppose that they are not motivated by a fondness for white supremacy but by a long-held belief in the great Western traditions of
"color-blindness" and "objective merit." How do we evaluate the mean-
ing of these phrases and determine to what extent "reverse discrimination" departs from our history of neutral decision-making? The only way
is to examine the problem historically. But when we turn to the real
world, we find not centuries of color-blindness and objective merit but
centuries of racism, slavery and discrimination ravaging the communities
and life chances of millions of African-Americans and other racial minorities. The rhetoric of "color-blindness" and "merit" rises up now as an
argument against affirmative action but it is nothing less than ridiculous
as a description of how American society has worked in the past.

The originator of the color-blindness metaphor was Justice Harlan,
who employed it with great normative effect in his powerful dissenting
opinion in *Plessy v. Ferguson*, the 1896 case upholding a state's authority
to segregate the races into "separate but equal" public accommodations.
Justice Harlan's famous words were: "Our constitution is color-blind, and

neither knows nor tolerates classes among citizens. In respect of civil rights, all citizens are equal before the law." This commonly quoted passage from his opinion demonstrates his analysis that the Constitution does not "permit any public authority to know the race of those entitled to be protected in the enjoyment of [civil] rights." According to Justice Harlan, the enactment of the 13th, 14th and 15th amendments swept out of the Constitution all legal sanction for racial oppression.

Stepped-up race-conscious affirmative action by all of our principal institutions must be taken in order to integrate and liberate American society.

From the standpoint of the debate about affirmative action today, there are several things to notice about Justice Harlan's dissenting opinion. In the first place, it never casts doubt on the validity of legislation and policy designed to *benefit*, as opposed to harm, the black population. The facts of the case—forced race segregation on railway trains—obviously did not raise this issue, but the none-too-remote example of pro-black Reconstruction programs was readily available if Justice Harlan had wanted to make his "color-blindness" argument seem more evenhanded and thus more palatable and compelling to his colleagues. But he did not seize upon such evidence. On the contrary, his opinion evinces clear recognition that the purpose of the Reconstruction constitutional amendments was "to secure 'to a race recently emancipated, a race that through many generations have been held in slavery, all the civil rights that the superior race enjoy.'"

In this sense, Justice Harlan saw that the constitutional principles establishing "color-blindness" were accomplished by the struggle for black rights and in order to uplift the black community. He had no problem recognizing that the Constitution was explicitly race-conscious about protecting the rights of the freedmen against discrimination, violence and tyranny by whites in power. And these rights were not merely formal ones: in the late-19th century, as William Forbath has argued, the Constitution was seen to grant citizens substantive rights to enjoy an economic and social livelihood through productive work.

Thus, it is an error to uproot the positive idea of color-blindness from the struggle against white supremacy and racial domination. As Randall Kennedy has written about the call for color-blindness in the twentieth-century civil rights movement:

> [I]t appears that the concept of race-blindness was simply a proxy for the fundamental demand that racial subjugation be eradicated. This demand . . . focused upon the condition of racial subjugation; its target was not only procedures that overtly excluded Negroes on the basis of race, but also the self-perpetuating dynamics of subordination that had survived the demise of American apartheid. The opponents of affirmative action have stripped the historical context from the demand for race-blind law. They have fashioned this demand into a new totem and insist on deference to it no matter what its effects upon the very group the fourteenth amendment was created to protect.

A second crucial point is that Justice Harlan believed that the statute in question in *Plessy*—a Louisiana law requiring the segregation of the races in railway travel—unlawfully imposed a stamp of inferiority and degradation on black citizens. As he wrote: "What can more certainly arouse race hate, what more certainly create and perpetuate a feeling of distrust between these races, than state enactments which, in fact, proceed on the ground that colored citizens are so inferior and degraded that they cannot be allowed to sit in public coaches occupied by white citizens?"

Indeed, far from resting his opinion on the fourteenth amendment alone, Justice Harlan repeatedly invoked the authority of the *thirteenth* amendment ban on involuntary servitude. He stated: "The arbitrary separation of citizens, on the basis of race, while they are on a public highway, is a badge of servitude wholly inconsistent with the civil freedom and the equality before the law established by the constitution." Thus, if we want to take Justice Harlan's opinion seriously and use it with a sense of historical proportion, it is very difficult to characterize educational or occupational affirmative action for African-Americans as a "badge of servitude" pasted on whites.

Color-blindness and white supremacy

Having said all of this, however, the absolutely crucial point overlooked (but perhaps not) by contemporary champions of "color-blindness" is that Justice Harlan did not view the legal principle of color-blindness as in any way inconsistent with the institution and perpetuation of white supremacy. The rhetoric of legal color-blindness flowed directly out of the conviction that whites could maintain their absolute dominance in society, government and economy without resorting to legal apartheid. Consider the haunting sentences which immediately preceded Justice Harlan's famous formulation:

> The white race deems itself to be the dominant race in this country. And so it is, in prestige, in achievements, in education, in wealth, and in power. So, I doubt not, it will continue to be for all time, if it remains true to its great heritage, and holds fast to the principles of constitutional liberty. But in view of the constitution, in the eye of the law, there is in this country no superior, dominant, ruling class of citizens. There is no caste here. Our constitution is color-blind.

Justice Harlan apparently believed that continuing white control of cultural institutions ("prestige" and "achievements"), universities ("education"), corporations and employment ("wealth") and government ("power") would permit the indefinite continuation of *de facto* white supremacy in a legally color-blind American society. (Incidentally, he also appeared to have no problem with discrimination, *de jure* or *de facto*, against "the Chinese race.") Thus, even if we (generously) assume that Justice Harlan's vision of color-blindness was intended to foreclose efforts like affirmative action, the vision itself would be morally and politically incomplete—if not indefensible—from a modern perspective since it was defined, at its very inception, as perfectly consistent with perpetual white supremacy in American society.

Finally, current invocation of color-blindness as a standard for policy judgment obscures the fact that Justice Harlan's argument lost: his opinion in *Plessy* was a dissent. This fact is important for two reasons. First, the Supreme Court never adopted the doctrinal language of color-blindness. The *Plessy* doctrine of separate-but-equal was effectively interred when the Supreme Court rendered its decision in *Brown v. Board of Education*. But the *Brown* Court did not adopt the categorical position of constitutional color-blindness. Rather, it rested its invalidation of school segregation on the empirical premise that "[s]eparate educational facilities are inherently unequal." The second point to remember is that, because Justice Harlan was in the minority, Jim Crow [racial segregation] laws lasted up until at least 1954 and no real forward movement in terms of dismantling social apartheid took place until enactment of the Civil Rights Act of 1964 and the Voting Rights Act of 1965. Since then, there has been progress in lifting up the African-American community from the disadvantages and disabilities imposed by hundreds of years of slavery, racism, violence, discrimination, bigotry, and ridicule—but we are a long way from racial equality and real justice for all communities.

And here we get to the heart of the matter. The critics of affirmative action invite us to believe that we live in a color-blind society in which the last vestige of racial discrimination is affirmative action itself. This extraordinary vision of American society simply cannot be squared with the facts of how whites and racial minorities live, how much they earn and what kind of wealth and power they have. The grim statistics of disparity force us to choose between the hideous "Bell Curve" vision of various races having differing aptitudes and the far more plausible conclusion that different ethnic and racial communities have equal potential to flourish but different levels of access to wealth, power and the good life. Surely as a society we should choose the second interpretation as a matter of both empirical belief and moral faith. If we believe in the equal potential of all human beings and we therefore cannot justify the dominance of the "white race" over all others "in prestige, in achievements, in education, in wealth, and in power," then stepped-up race-conscious affirmative action by all of our principal institutions must be taken in order to integrate and liberate American society.

The meaning of meritocracy

This assertion, however, leads us directly to the conservatives' central argument: that affirmative action undermines the regime of merit, which requires neutral distribution of social rewards according to objective criteria. Even just restating the argument begins to erode confidence in it because it is so obvious that each of its key terms is wholly empty outside of the processes of historical definition. Merit is neither self-defining nor self-revealing; it is an ever-changing concept that is historically, socially and institutionally contingent—and often contested. It is impossible to define merit without asking what kinds of institutions we want to have and for what purposes. As Stanley Fish writes, "merit is not an abstract, independent standard but one that follows from the traditions and practices of a community whose presuppositions are not at the moment the object of scrutiny or skepticism." Once a particular conception of "merit" is challenged, it may be revised and transformed until the new conception is itself overthrown and the process repeats itself. The words that inevitably follow in the rhetorical train of "merit," such as "neutral" and "objective," are either totally abstract and empty or, in the real world, transparently loaded down with the freight of particular historical, social, political and institutional meanings.

Merit is not an abstract, independent standard but one that follows from the traditions and practices of a community.

Consider the example of law schools. A century ago, they had, roughly speaking, all-white, all-male faculties and all-white, all-male student bodies. The criteria then used for admission—race, gender, college attended, grades, family and social connections—worked to reproduce an elite bar that served the legal needs of emerging large-scale corporate capitalism. That system was not really altered until the Law School Admissions Test (LSAT) was introduced a few decades ago and agitation for social change lowered barriers for women and minorities to enter. At each step, voices were heard to say that neutral definitions of "merit" were being diluted in favor of some diluting trend.

But what qualities now warrant admission to law school? One can think of dozens: the extent to which a person would make an excellent brief-writer; the extent to which a person would make an excellent oral advocate; the extent to which a person would make a great legal scholar or great legal teacher; how well a person has performed on standardized exams, including the LSAT; the extent to which a person would enrich discussion in class; the extent to which the person has overcome adversity and demonstrates determination to succeed; the extent to which the person has empathy and compassion for people in vulnerable positions; the extent to which the person is part of a community in which she could find clients; how much business background a person has; the extent to which a person volunteers and serves others; the extent to which the person received good grades in college in law-related subjects; the quality of the application essays; the extent to which the person received good grades in college generally or in high school or in elementary school; the extent to which the person has worked during school, or worked in a law-related capacity; the extent to which the person is likely to go to a large law firm and give the law school large contributions as an alumnus; the extent to which the person will work to serve the poor and disempowered and thus bring recognition and praise to the law school; the extent to which a person will uplift an historically oppressed community through creative legal tactics—or keep it down through the same; the extent to which the person will use law to promote or undermine environmental protection; the extent to which the person has had the benefit (or hindrance) of coming from a family of lawyers or being the first person in her family even to apply to law school; and so on *ad infinitum*.

Each of these criteria presents itself as a perfectly plausible consideration for law school admission today. How to choose among them? Surely it comes down to the school's self-definition and conscious (or unconscious) institutional project. But it is unlikely that any law school actually narrows its criteria down to just a few of these to the exclusion of all others. Rather, my experience has been that members of admissions committees tend to proceed on a series of general assumptions and hunches that incorporate all of these considerations and respond more or less idiosyncratically to the rationales for admission presented by an applicant's paperwork. Of course, many law schools place heaviest emphasis on college grades and LSAT scores but these should not be controlling criteria since neither is perfectly predictive of "success" and both are flawed in important ways. Of the two, grades appear to have a better capacity to predict "performance" in law school, but then again law school performance itself is defined with respect to grades, and who is to say that law students with better grades end up making better lawyers?

LSAT scores may best reflect whether the student took an LSAT preparation course, which are guaranteed to raise your score by 10 or 12 points or you get your money back. Of course, not everyone has the money or the time to take such a course. There are also a host of questions about whether a high-pressure, carefully-timed competitive multiple-choice examination is the best way to test someone's ability to make a good and productive lawyer. The skills that permit someone to excel on such a test may predict how well they do on the bar exam or even how they would be as an associate at a large corporate law firm. But how well does excellence at taking the LSAT predict whether the person will work for justice, serve her community, exercise wisdom or change our way of looking at important legal issues?

Speaking personally, I favor a progressive lessening of reliance on the LSAT and a loosening of compulsive and unreflective attitudes about grades. But even schools that place most emphasis on the LSAT and grades do not use them exclusively; even they include room for discretion and judgment by admissions committee members. Thus, as soon as we stray from the illusive clarity of numerical criteria, we are thrown into the realm of value judgments about what kinds of institutions we want to create and what kinds of purposes we want them to serve. Is there something illegitimate about recognizing race, gender, ethnicity and socioeconomic background in this process?

No escape from race-consciousness

The first point to make is that it is almost impossible not to take these factors into account without closing your eyes. When a law school applicant puts down on her application that she has spent the last three years raising her children, or that he spent twenty hours a week working his way through college, or that her parents are immigrants from Thailand, or that English is his second language, or that she was college vice-president of the Hispanic Students Association, or that she plans to work as a civil rights lawyer because her brother was a victim of race discrimination, or that she lives on an Indian reservation and plans to return there, then the complicated social facts of race, gender, class and ethnicity—which are partially constitutive of all of us as individuals—leap off the page and make themselves part of the consciousness of the admissions decision.

These facts that are so wrapped up with our selves cannot be blinked away; they inform admissions deliberations at every turn. If a student is poor, does his hard work as a pizza delivery person count in his favor or does the related fact that he had no meaningful extracurricular activities outside of work count against him? How should his summer delivering pizza be measured against a wealthier student's summer working as a paralegal at a law firm or volunteering at a homeless shelter? Does an applicant's knowledge of English as a second language suggest that law school will be too difficult for her or that she will be able to serve a lawyer-poor language minority community? Should a family full of lawyers be used to indicate likely success in law school and in finding a job or should it be used to discount the significance of the applicant's superb essay dealing with constitutional law? It is absurd to think that race, gender, and class ever were—or ever could be—"irrelevant" to the admissions process, which is all about making value judgments and deeply political choices.

Historical and political imperative

But if they are not—and cannot be—irrelevant, should the factors of race, gender, ethnicity and class actually work to the benefit of racial minorities, women and non-affluent people? Surely they should. This judgment is a pragmatic one based on both history and politics.

The American historical record of racial domination—including slavery, ruthless violence, labor exploitation, disenfranchisement, employment and housing discrimination, theft, destruction of communities and families, school segregation, Jim Crow laws, unemployment, and injustice—also includes the less dramatic but systematic use of quotas and affirmative action for white men in every major profession, university, discipline, trade and so on. For centuries, the criteria of race, gender, ethnicity and class worked to benefit particular groups and to keep other groups down. The only way to counteract the pervasive exclusionary impact of such practices on women and minorities is to consciously bring them into institutions which have so long shut them out. One can view this as a kind of historical reparation and democratic rectification of the one-sided development of American institutions.

How well does excellence at taking the LSAT predict whether the person will work for justice, serve her community, exercise wisdom?

Politically, it can only make sense to practice meaningful affirmative action. We live in a society in which group subordination is still pervasive and the patterns and prospects of human lives are substantially determined by the facts of race, ethnicity, and gender. Unless we want to descend to the level of tribal conflict and competition seen in Bosnia or Lebanon, then Duncan Kennedy is right that "we should be a culturally pluralist society that deliberately structures institutions so that communities and social classes share wealth and power." Without this sharing process, a multicultural society begins to live on processes of formal or informal apartheid, domination and coercion, bitter resentment and rage, and false superiority and hubris. If we are going to live together harmoniously, cultural pluralism "means that we should structure the competition of racial and ethnic communities and social classes in markets and bureaucracies, and in the political system, in such a way that no community or class is systematically subordinated."

It is absurd to think that race, gender, and class ever were—or ever could be—"irrelevant" to the admissions process.

Conservatives argue that this process of intentionally sharing social goods among various groups is demeaning or, in their favorite phrase, "stigmatizing." There may be a real concern here to be watched, but surely the benefits of affirmative action to racial minorities or women now far outweigh such risks. Or, to put it differently, if our concern is stigma and self-doubt, then let us trust minorities and women *themselves* to declare when the bad of affirmative action outweighs the good. Most people know that those whites who are prone to think ill of minorities don't need affirmative action as an excuse to do it. At any rate, it is certainly hard to trust conservatives on this point when they have maligned minorities for so long. Indeed, part and parcel of the anti-PC project today is the defense, in far more than formal terms, of various hate speakers, pseudoscientific calumny against minorities, and the relentless ridicule of various minority and women scholars. Conservatives could do a lot more to de-stigmatize the beneficiaries of affirmative action simply by calling off the war on "political correctness" and ceasing speculation about hereditary mental differences.

The Civil Rights movement and affirmative action

At any rate, in defending affirmative action, it is necessary to go beyond the idea of sharing power and resources in a culturally plural society. It is essential to recall the political and spiritual project of the modern Civil Rights movement that made affirmative action both necessary and possible. The Civil Rights movement never had as its conscious political project the creation of "affirmative action" or "set-aside" programs in various white-controlled institutions like universities, corporations, and labor unions. Affirmative action, rather, came about as part of the dominant society's effort to respond to the movement's growing insistence on fundamental social change to end oppressive conditions pervasive in the African-American community.

Affirmative action in the sense it is used today played no real role in the political program or rhetoric of Reverend Martin Luther King or the Southern Christian Leadership Conference, which was struggling to bring down American apartheid and secure the right to vote. Nor was it a theme in the work of the Student Non-Violent Coordinating Committee, which was organizing grassroots voter registration drives and freedom schools throughout the South. Nor did affirmative action figure at all in the rhetoric or program of Malcolm X or the Black Panthers, whose demand for "black power" was a call for black-controlled institutions—not little pieces of white institutions.

But if affirmative action had little or no presence in the political project of the Civil Rights movement, the movement was the necessary condition for the creation of affirmative action. For "affirmative action" in fact began in 1961 with President John F. Kennedy's 1961 Executive Order instructing federal contractors "to at least make sure," as he put it, "that we are giving everyone a fair chance." This gentle admonition came as part of the Kennedy administration's grudging response to civil rights organizing in the black communities of the South.

It is thus important to see the essential conservatism and modesty of affirmative action as it first appeared. The Civil Rights movement favored sweeping interracial social change: racial desegregation in schools and housing, federal protection of the right to vote, a massive redirection of public funds from spending on warfare and military preparation to social needs, an end to poverty and a reduction in social inequality, community control of schools, radical upgrading of public goods like health, welfare and housing, higher wages and labor power, and a moral and spiritual renewal of a culture descending into the nightmare of violence and hatred.

But the Johnson administration's Executive Order 11246 provides a nice sense of the relative insignificance of affirmative action: "The contractor will take affirmative action to ensure that applicants are employed, and that employees are treated during employment, without regard to their race, color, religion, sex, or national origin." Affirmative action was thus a baby-step toward progress: an incremental, forward-looking counterweight to institutionalized white privilege. But it was nothing close to the solutions needed to transform America.

Thus, if affirmative action seemed a mild palliative, it also seemed perfectly secure and logical. It was buttressed and protected by a people *in motion*: an aroused African-American community and a radical social change politics demanding immediate social progress. Affirmative action to open the doors of government—and later business and universities—seemed the least that could be done to soften (if not forestall) the more sweeping changes that were in the air. A kind of top-down bureaucratic invitation to join the mainstream at entry levels, affirmative action was a completely logical response to a movement of a people demanding their long-denied rights to participate fully in the American polity, society and economy.

Affirmative action was a completely logical response to a movement of a people demanding their long-denied rights to participate fully in the American polity.

It is a measure of both the vanishing of a popular energized Civil Rights movement and the nation's economic retraction that this modest program, seen as so unassuming and unobjectionable at the beginning, is now reviled in many places, deeply controversial and profoundly vulnerable. Thus, progressives who ought to be promoting far more radical proposals to reduce class power and race inequality in America are left holding the bag for a program designed by the establishment to assimilate social changes in a safe way and at a cautious speed.

Affirmative action made sense to the public in the context of a series of challenges to the distribution of power, wealth, recognition, and income in American society. To the extent that people understood the Civil Rights movement as a political assault on the naturalness and legitimacy of various social processes and outcomes, affirmative action appeared to be a perfectly sensible and incremental way to realign institutional outcomes rigged and distorted by racism. But, today, without the vision of an active Civil Rights movement exposing the racial, gender and class construction of "meritocracy" under a regime of white male supremacy, affirmative action seems abberational and bizarre. If one passively accepts the assumption that there is nothing wrong with the way wealth and power are distributed in America (but minorities and women need to be included in various elites) and that American power elites are operating in the best interests of all citizens (but minorities and women need a fair chance to get to the top too), then the political logic of affirmative action rapidly shrinks and takes on more of the character of special pleading. In political terms, working-class whites who do not enjoy the benefits of class society will see little reason to endorse a program which is simply about integrating various political and economic elites that dominate wealth and power. Because the overall legitimacy of the meritocracy is implicitly being affirmed, they are, in effect, being told that the reason they are stuck at the bottom is that they lack the merit to succeed.

Reviving affirmative action

We need a defense of affirmative action that links up with a thoroughgoing critique of American meritocracy and power relationships. We need to revive a progressive challenge to the background social assumptions about education and employment in America: that higher education is for the elite only and should not be free to the people; that privately created and administered standardized exams are the best way to ascertain merit and distribute students across various levels of colleges; that the best teachers should teach the best students; that no one has a right to a job or productive work; that extreme hierarchy and role-division is inherent in the workplace; that radical disparities between the wages of people who handle things and people who handle words are natural and necessary; that work commonly done by women is inherently less worthy than work commonly done by men; that unions are an albatross and must be as authoritarian as employers; and that the society must operate on the principle of constant and fierce individual competition or else face ineluctable economic decline.

In short, to transcend the destructive politics of division and derision surrounding affirmative action (if we still can), we need to reaffirm the equality of all peoples in a culturally pluralist society and to posit a universal politics of freedom and equality for the next century. But a vigorous defense of affirmative action right now is central to such a politics. For in a society where the lines of race and gender double as lines of class and power, even the idea of affirmative action for minorities and women is an affront to the structure of domination and inequality. Our job must be to make affirmative action the first line of defense in a politics which insists that all citizens have a right to equal participation in the fruits of our social life.

4

Society Needs Affirmative Action Based on Class, Not Race

Richard Kahlenberg

Richard Kahlenberg, a contributor to the New Republic, *a politically liberal weekly newsmagazine, is the author of a book about class-based affirmative action.*

Because the survival of affirmative action is threatened by those opposed to racial preferences, the programs should be revamped to address class-based inequities. Such an approach has already proven workable in a number of universities. By focusing on non-racial criteria that impact everyone regardless of skin color or ethnicity, this policy unifies those of disparate groups and thereby functions as an effective tool for battling racism. The legacy of racism has placed disproportionate numbers of minorities among the disadvantaged; class-based preferences could become a more effective means of assisting those with the greatest need within each minority group. Shifting from issues of race to those of poverty also furthers the vision of civil rights leader Martin Luther King Jr., who sought to unite the poor of all races.

In an act that reflected panic as much as cool reflection, Bill Clinton said that he is reviewing all federal affirmative action programs to see "whether there is some other way we can reach [our] objective without giving a preference by race or gender." As the country's mood swings violently against affirmative action, and as Republicans gear up to use the issue to bludgeon the Democratic coalition yet again in 1996, the whole project of legislating racial equality seems suddenly in doubt. The Democrats, terrified of the issue, are now hoping it will just go away. It won't. But at every political impasse, there is a political opportunity. Bill Clinton has a chance, as no other Democrat has had since 1968, to turn a glaring liability for his party into an advantage—without betraying basic Democratic principles.

Richard Kahlenberg, "Class, Not Race," *The New Republic*, April 3, 1995. Reprinted by permission of *The New Republic*; © 1995, The New Republic, Inc.

Redeeming affirmative action

There is, as Clinton said, a way "we can work this out." But it isn't the "*Bakke* straddle," which says yes to affirmative action (race as a factor) but no to quotas [*Bakke* is a 1978 Supreme Court ruling against racial discrimination in school admissions]. It isn't William Julius Wilson's call to "emphasize" race-neutral social programs, while downplaying affirmative action. The days of downplaying are gone; we can count on the Republicans for that. The way out—an idea Clinton hinted at—is to introduce the principle of race neutrality and the goal of aiding the disadvantaged into affirmative action preference programs themselves: to base preferences, in education, entry-level employment and public contracting, on class, not race.

Were Clinton to propose this move, the media would charge him with lurching to the right. Jesse Jackson's presidential campaign would surely soon follow. But despite its association with conservatives such as Clarence Thomas, Antonin Scalia and Dinesh D'Souza, the idea of class-based affirmative action should in fact appeal to the left as well. After all, its message of addressing class unfairness and its political potential for building cross-racial coalitions are traditional liberal staples.

Class, not race

For many years, the left argued not only that class was important, but also that it was more important than race. This argument was practical, ideological and politic. An emphasis on class inequality meant Robert Kennedy riding in a motorcade through cheering white and black sections of racially torn Gary, Indiana, in 1968, with black Mayor Richard Hatcher on one side, and white working-class boxing hero Tony Zale on the other.

Ideologically, it was clear that with the passage of the Civil Rights Act of 1964, class replaced caste as the central impediment to equal opportunity. Martin Luther King Jr. moved from the Montgomery Boycott [which protested racial segregation on city buses] to the Poor People's Campaign [which advocated anti-poverty laws], which he described as "his last, greatest dream," and "something bigger than just a civil rights movement for Negroes." Robert Kennedy told David Halberstam that "it was pointless to talk about the real problem in America being black and white, it was really rich and poor, which was a much more complex subject."

The priority given to race over class has inevitably exacerbated white racism.

Finally, the left emphasized class because to confuse class and race was seen not only as wrong but as dangerous. This notion was at the heart of the protest over Daniel Patrick Moynihan's 1965 report, *The Negro Family: The Case for National Action*, in which Moynihan depicted the rising rates of illegitimacy among poor blacks. While Moynihan's critics were wrong to silence discussion of illegitimacy among blacks, they rightly noted that the title of the report, which implicated all blacks, was misleading, and that fairly high rates of illegitimacy also were present among poor whites—a point which Moynihan readily endorses today. (In the wake of the second set of Los Angeles riots in 1992, Moynihan rose on the Senate floor to reaffirm that family structure "is not an issue of race but of class. . . . It is class behavior.")

The irony is that affirmative action based on race violates these three liberal insights. It provides the ultimate wedge to destroy Robert Kennedy's coalition. It says that despite civil rights protections, the wealthiest African American is more deserving of preference than the poorest white. It relentlessly focuses all attention on race.

In contrast, Lyndon Johnson's June 1965 address to Howard University, in which the concept of affirmative action was first unveiled, did not ignore class. In a speech drafted by Moynihan, Johnson spoke of the bifurcation of the black community, and, in his celebrated metaphor, said we needed to aid those "hobbled" in life's race by past discrimination. This suggested special help for disadvantaged blacks, not all blacks; for the young Clarence Thomas, but not for Clarence Thomas's son. Johnson balked at implementing the thematic language of his speech. His Executive Order 11246, calling for "affirmative action" among federal contractors, initially meant greater outreach and required hiring without respect to race. In fact, Johnson rescinded his Labor Department's proposal to provide for racial quotas in the construction industry in Philadelphia. It fell to Richard Nixon to implement the "Philadelphia Plan," in what Nixon's aides say was a conscious effort to drive a wedge between blacks and labor. (Once he placed racial preferences on the table, Nixon adroitly extricated himself, and by 1972 was campaigning against racial quotas.)

The ironies were compounded by the Supreme Court. In the 1974 case *DeFunis* v. *Odegaard*, in which a system of racial preferences in law school admissions was at issue, it was the Court's liberal giant, William O. Douglas, who argued that racial preferences were unconstitutional, and suggested instead that preferences be based on disadvantage. Four years later, in the *Bakke* case, the great proponent of affirmative action as a means to achieve "diversity" was Nixon appointee Lewis F. Powell Jr. Somewhere along the line, the right wing embraced Douglas and Critical Race Theory embraced Powell.

Overlooking the disadvantaged

Today, the left pushes racial preferences, even for the most advantaged minorities, in order to promote diversity and provide role models for disadvantaged blacks—an argument which, if it came from Ronald Reagan, the left would rightly dismiss as trickle-down social theory. Today, when William Julius Wilson argues the opposite of the Moynihan report—that the problems facing the black community are rooted more in class than race—it is Wilson who is excoriated by civil rights groups. The left can barely utter the word "class," instead resorting to euphemisms such as "income groups," "wage earners" and "people who play by the rules."

For all of this, the left has paid a tremendous price. On a political level, with a few notable exceptions, the history of the past twenty-five years is a history of white, working-class Robert Kennedy Democrats turning first into Wallace Democrats, then into Nixon and Reagan Democrats and ultimately into today's Angry White Males. Time and again, the white working class votes its race rather than its class, and Republicans win. The failure of the left to embrace class also helps turn poor blacks, for whom racial preferences are, in Stephen Carter's words, "stunningly irrelevant," toward Louis Farrakhan [leader of the Nation of Islam].

It is possible to devise an enforceable set of objective standards for deprivation.

On the merits, the left has committed itself to a goal—equality of group results—which seems highly radical, when it is in fact rather unambitious. To the extent that affirmative action, at its ultimate moment of success, merely creates a self-perpetuating black elite along with a white one, its goal is modest—certainly more conservative than real equality of opportunity, which gives blacks and whites and other Americans of all economic strata a fair chance at success.

The priority given to race over class has inevitably exacerbated white racism. Today, both liberals and conservatives conflate race and class because it serves both of their purposes to do so. Every year, when SAT [Scholastic Assessment Test] scores are released, the breakdown by race shows enormous gaps between blacks on the one hand and whites and Asians on the other. The NAACP [National Association for the Advancement of Colored People] cites these figures as evidence that we need to do more. Charles Murray cites the same statistics as evidence of intractable racial differences. We rarely see a breakdown of scores by class, which would show enormous gaps between rich and poor, gaps that would help explain the differences in scores by race.

On the legal front, it once made some strategic sense to emphasize race over class. But when states moved to the remedial phrase—and began trying to address past discrimination—the racial focus became a liability. The strict scrutiny that struck down Jim Crow [racial segregation laws] is now used, to varying degrees, to curtail racial preferences. Class, on the other hand, is not one of the suspect categories under the Fourteenth Amendment, which leaves class-based remedies much less assailable.

Class-based programs work

If class-based affirmative action is a theory that liberals should take seriously, how would it work in practice? Magazine editor Michael Kinsley has asked, "Does Clarence Thomas, the sharecropper's kid, get more or fewer preference points than the unemployed miner's son from Appalachia?" Most conservative proponents of class-based affirmative action have failed to explain their idea with any degree of specificity. Either they're insincere—offering the alternative only for tactical reasons—or they're stumped.

The former is more likely. While the questions of implementation are serious and difficult, they are not impossible to answer. At the university level, admissions committees deal every day with precisely the type of apples-and-oranges question that Kinsley poses. Should a law school admit an applicant with a 3.2 GPA [grade point average] from Yale or a 3.3 from Georgetown? How do you compare those two if one applicant worked for the Peace Corps but the other had slightly higher LSATs [Law School Admissions Test]?

In fact, a number of universities already give preferences for disadvantaged students in addition to racial minorities. Since 1989 the University of California at Berkeley has granted special consideration to applicants "from socioeconomically disadvantaged backgrounds . . . regardless of race or ethnicity." Temple University Law School has, since the 1970s, given preference to "applicants who have overcome exceptional and continuous economic deprivation." And at Hastings College of Law, 20 percent of the class is set aside for disadvantaged students through the Legal Equal Opportunity Program. Even the University of California-Davis medical program challenged by Allan Bakke was limited to "disadvantaged" minorities, a system which Davis apparently did not find impossible to administer.

Similar class-based preference programs could be provided by public employers and federal contractors for high school graduates not pursuing college, on the theory that at that age their class-based handicaps hide their true potential and are not at all of their own making. In public contracting, government agencies could follow the model of New York City's old class-based program, which provided preferences based not on the ethnicity or gender of the contractor, but to small firms located in New York City which did part of their business in depressed areas or employed economically disadvantaged workers.

The definition of class or disadvantage may vary according to context, but if, for example, the government chose to require class-based affirmative action from universities receiving federal funds, it is possible to devise an enforceable set of objective standards for deprivation. If the aim of class-based affirmative action is to provide a system of genuine equality of opportunity, a leg up to promising students who have done well despite the odds, we have a wealth of sociological data to devise an obstacles test. While some might balk at the very idea of reducing disadvantage to a number, we currently reduce intellectual promise to numbers—SATs and GPAs—and adding a number for disadvantage into the calculus just makes deciding who gets ahead and who does not a little fairer.

Determining factors

There are three basic ways to proceed: with a simple, moderate or complex definition. The simple method is to ask college applicants their family's income and measure disadvantage by that factor alone, on the theory that income is a good proxy for a whole host of economic disadvantages (such as bad schools or a difficult learning environment). This oversimplified approach is essentially the tack we've taken with respect to compensatory race-based affirmative action. For example, most affirmative action programs ask applicants to check a racial box and sweep all the ambiguities under the rug. Even though African Americans have, as Justice Thurgood Marshall said in *Bakke*, suffered a history "different in kind, not just degree, from that of other ethnic groups," universities don't calibrate preferences based on comparative group disadvantage (and, in the Davis system challenged by Bakke, two-thirds of the preferences went to Mexican-Americans and Asians, not blacks). We also ignore the question of when an individual's family immigrated in order to determine whether the family was even theoretically subject to the of-

ficial discrimination in this country on which preferences are predicated.
"Diversity" was supposed to solve all this by saying we don't care about compensation, only viewpoint. But, again, if universities are genuinely seeking diversity of viewpoints, they should inquire whether a minority applicant really does have the "minority viewpoint" being sought. Derrick Bell's famous statement—"the ends of diversity are not served by people who look black and think white"—is at once repellent and a relevant critique of the assumption that all minority members think alike. In theory, we need some assurance from the applicant that he or she will in fact interact with students of different backgrounds, lest the cosmetic diversity of the freshman yearbook be lost to the reality of ethnic theme houses.

There appears to be a societal consensus . . . that kids from poor backgrounds deserve a leg up.

The second way to proceed, the moderately complicated calculus of class, would look at what sociologists believe to be the Big Three determinants of life chances: parental income, education and occupation. Parents' education, which is highly correlated with a child's academic achievement, can be measured in number of years. And while ranking occupations might seem hopelessly complex, various attempts to do so objectively have yielded remarkably consistent results—from the Barr Scale of the early 1920s to Alba Edwards' Census rankings of the 1940s to the Duncan Scores of the 1960s.

The third alternative, the complex calculus of disadvantage, would count all the factors mentioned, but might also look at net worth, the quality of secondary education, neighborhood influences and family structure. An applicant's family wealth is readily available from financial aid forms, and provides a long-term view of relative disadvantage, to supplement the "snapshot" picture that income provides. We also know that schooling opportunities are crucial to a student's life chances, even controlling for home environment. Some data suggest that a disadvantaged student at a middle-class school does better on average than a middle-class student at a school with high concentrations of poverty. Objective figures are available to measure secondary school quality—from per student expenditure, to the percentage of students receiving free or reduced-price lunches, to a school's median score on standardized achievement tests. Neighborhood influences, measured by the concentration of poverty within Census tracts or zip codes, could also be factored in, since numerous studies have found that living in a low-income community can adversely affect an individual's life chances above and beyond family income. Finally, everyone from [former Republican vice president] Dan Quayle to Donna Shalala [secretary of health and human services for the Clinton administration] agrees that children growing up in single-parent homes have a tougher time. This factor could be taken into account as well.

The point is not that this list is the perfect one, but that it *is* possible to devise a series of fairly objective and verifiable factors that measure the degree to which a teenager's true potential has been hidden. (As it happens, the complex definition is the one that disproportionately benefits

African Americans. Even among similar income groups, blacks are more likely than whites to live in concentrated poverty, go to bad schools and live in single-parent homes.) It's just not true that a system of class preferences is inherently harder to administer than a system based on race. Race only seems simpler because we have ignored the ambiguities. And racial preferences are just as easy to ridicule. To paraphrase Kinsley, does a new Indian immigrant get fewer or more points than a third-generation Latino whose mother is Anglo?

Who should benefit? Mickey Kaus, in his magazine article, "Class Is In," argued that class preferences should be reserved for the underclass. But the injuries of class extend beyond the poorest. The offspring of the working poor and the working class lack advantages, too, and indeed SAT scores correlate lockstep with income at every increment. Unless you believe in genetic inferiority, these statistics suggest unfairness is not confined to the underclass. As a practical matter, a teenager who emerges from the underclass has little chance of surviving at an elite college. At Berkeley, administrators found that using a definition of disadvantaged, under which neither parent attended a four-year college and the family could not afford to pay $1,000 in education expenses, failed to bring in enough students who were likely to pass.

Addressing objections

Still, there are several serious objections to class-based preferences that must be addressed.

1. *We're not ready to be color-blind because racial discrimination continues to afflict our society*. Ron Brown says affirmative action "continues to be needed not to redress grievances of the past, but the current discrimination that continues to exist." This is a relatively new theory, which conveniently elides the fact that preferences were supposed to be temporary. It also stands logic on its head. While racial discrimination undoubtedly still exists, the Civil Rights Act of 1964 was meant to address prospective discrimination. Affirmative action—discrimination in itself—makes sense only to the extent that there is a current-day legacy of *past* discrimination which new prospective laws cannot reach back and remedy.

In the contexts of education and employment, the Civil Rights Act already contains powerful tools to address intentional and unintentional discrimination. The Civil Rights Act of 1991 reaffirmed the need to address unintentional discrimination—by requiring employers to justify employment practices that are statistically more likely to hurt minorities—but it did so without crossing the line to required preferences. This principle also applies to Title VI of the Civil Rights Act, so that if, for example, it can be shown that the SAT produces an unjustified disparate impact, a university can be barred from using it. In addition, "soft" forms of affirmative action, which require employers and universities to broaden the net and interview people from all races, are good ways of ensuring positions are not filled by word of mouth, through wealthy white networks.

We have weaker tools to deal with discrimination in other areas of life—say, taxi drivers who refuse to pick up black businessmen—but how does a preference in education or employment remedy that wrong? By contrast, there is nothing illegal about bad schools, bad housing and grossly stunted opportunities for the poor. A class preference is perfectly appropriate.

2. *Class preferences will be just as stigmatizing as racial preferences.* Michael Kinsley argues that "any debilitating self-doubt that exists because of affirmative action is not going to be mitigated by being told you got into Harvard because of your 'socioeconomic disadvantage' rather than your race." But class preferences are different from racial preferences in at least two important respects. First, stigma—in one's own eyes and the eyes of others—is bound up with the question of whether an admissions criterion is accepted as legitimate. Students with good grades aren't seen as getting in "just because they're smart." And there appears to be a societal consensus—from Douglas to Scalia—that kids from poor backgrounds deserve a leg up. Such a consensus has never existed for class-blind racial preferences.

Second, there is no myth of inferiority in this country about the abilities of poor people comparable to that about African Americans. Now, if racial preferences are purely a matter of compensatory justice, then the question of whether preferences exacerbate white racism is not relevant. But today racial preferences are often justified by social utility (bringing different racial groups together helps dispel stereotypes) in which case the social consequences are highly relevant. The general argument made by proponents of racial preferences—that policies need to be grounded in social reality, not a historical theory—cuts in favor of the class category. Why? Precisely because there is no stubborn historical myth for it to reinforce.

Mickey Kaus makes a related argument when he says that class preferences "will still reward those who play the victim." But if objective criteria are used to define the disadvantaged, there is no way to "play" the victim. Poor and working-class teenagers are the victims of class inequality not of their own making. Preferences, unlike, say, a welfare check, tell poor teenagers not that they are helpless victims, but that we think their long-run potential is great, and we're going to give them a chance—if they work their tails off—to prove themselves.

The question is not whether we treat people as members of groups—that's inevitable—but whether the group is a relevant one.

---

3. *Class preferences continue to treat people as members of groups as opposed to individuals.* Yes. But so do university admissions policies that summarily reject students below a certain SAT level. It's hard to know what treating people as individuals means. (Perhaps if university admissions committees interviewed the teachers of each applicant back to kindergarten to get a better picture of their academic potential, we'd be treating them more as individuals.) The question is not whether we treat people as members of groups—that's inevitable—but whether the group is a relevant one. And in measuring disadvantage (and hidden potential) class is surely a much better proxy than race.

4. *Class-based affirmative action will not yield a diverse student body in elite colleges.* Actually, there is reason to believe that class preferences will disproportionately benefit people of color in most contexts—since mi-

norities are disproportionately poor. In the university context, however, class-based preferences were rejected during the 1970s in part because of fear that they would produce inadequate numbers of minority students. The problem is that when you control for income, African American students do worse than white and Asian students on the SAT—due in part to differences in culture and linguistic patterns, and in part to the way income alone as a measurement hides other class-based differences among ethnic groups.

The concern is a serious and complicated one. Briefly, there are four responses. First, even Murray and Richard Herrnstein agree that the residual racial gap in scores has declined significantly in the past two decades, so the concern, though real, is not as great as it once was. Second, if we use the sophisticated definition of class discussed earlier—which reflects the relative disadvantage of blacks vis-à-vis whites of the same income level—the racial gap should close further. Third, we can improve racial diversity by getting rid of unjustified preferences—for alumni kids or students from underrepresented geographic regions—which disproportionately hurt people of color. Finally, if the goal is to provide genuine equal opportunity, not equality of group result, and if we are satisfied that a meritocratic system which corrects for class inequality is the best possible approximation of that equality, then we have achieved our goal.

5. *Class-based affirmative action will cause as much resentment among those left out as race-based affirmative action.* Kinsley argues that the rejected applicant in the infamous Jesse Helms commercial from 1990 [which portrayed a white male losing a job to a less qualified minority applicant] would feel just as angry for losing out on a class-based as a race-based preference, since both involve "making up for past injustice." The difference, of course, is that class preferences go to the actual victims of class injury, mooting the whole question of intergenerational justice. In the racial context, this was called "victim specificity." Even the Reagan administration was in favor of compensating actual victims of racial discrimination.

The cheaper solution

The larger point implicit in Kinsley's question is a more serious one: that any preference system, whether race- or class-based, is "still a form of zero-sum social engineering." Why should liberals push for class preferences at all? Why not just provide more funding for education, safer schools, better nutrition? The answer is that liberals should do these things; but we cannot hold our breath for it to happen. In 1993, when all the planets were aligned—a populist Democratic president, Democratic control of both Houses of Congress—they produced what the *New York Times* called "A BUDGET WORTHY OF MR. BUSH." Cheaper alternatives, such as preferences, must supplement more expensive strategies of social spending. Besides, to the extent that class preferences help change the focus of public discourse from race to class, they help reforge the coalition needed to sustain the social programs liberals want.

Class preferences could restore the successful formula on which the early civil rights movement rested: morally unassailable underpinnings and a relatively inexpensive agenda. It's crucial to remember that Martin

Luther King Jr. called for special consideration based on class, not race. After laying out a forceful argument for the special debt owed to blacks, King rejected the call for a Negro Bill of Rights in favor of a Bill of Rights for the Disadvantaged. It was King's insight that there were nonracial ways to remedy racial wrongs, and that the injuries of class deserve attention along with the injuries of race.

None of this is to argue that King would have opposed affirmative action if the alternative were to do nothing. For Jesse Helms to invoke King's color-blind rhetoric now that it is in the interests of white people to do so is the worst kind of hypocrisy. Some form of compensation is necessary, and I think affirmative action, though deeply flawed, is better than nothing.

But the opportunity to save affirmative action of any kind may soon pass. If the Supreme Court continues to narrow the instances in which racial preferences are justified, if California voters put an end to affirmative action in their state and if Congress begins to roll back racial preferences in legislation which President Clinton finds hard to veto—or President Phil Gramm signs with gusto—conservatives will have less and less reason to bargain. Now is the time to call their bluff.

5

Affirmative Action Harms Black Professionals

Stephen L. Carter

Stephen L. Carter is the William Nelson Cromwell Professor of Law at Yale University and a self-described beneficiary of affirmative action. He has written numerous articles on racial issues, as well as the foreword for Lani Guinier's The Tyranny of the Majority, *and his own book,* Reflections of an Affirmative Action Baby, *from which this viewpoint is excerpted.*

Affirmative action undermines the achievements of blacks and other people of color by creating the perception that their positions were given to them rather than earned. Racial preferences are simply another form of racism, based on the assumption that blacks and other disadvantaged groups are intellectually inferior to whites and therefore incapable of success if held to the same standards. Such policies have given birth to the "best black" syndrome: the granting of special attention to a black individual of above average abilities only because she or he represents an aberration from racist stereotypes. Relegating these achievers to the ranks of the "best" within a minority group excludes them from being viewed as the best of the best drawn from the entire population.

Affirmative action has been with me always. I do not mean to suggest that I have always been the beneficiary of special programs and preferences. I mean, rather, that no matter what my accomplishments, I have had trouble escaping an assumption that often seems to underlie the worst forms of affirmative action: that black people cannot compete intellectually with white people. Certainly I have not escaped it since my teen years, spent mostly in Ithaca, New York, where the presence of Cornell University lends an air of academic intensity to the public schools. At Ithaca High School in the days of my adolescence, we had far more than our share of National Merit Scholars, of students who scored exceptionally well on standardized tests, of students who earned advanced placement credits for college, and of every other commodity by which secondary schools compare their academic quality.

Competing with the best

My father taught at Cornell, which made me a Cornell kid, a "fac-brat," and I hung out with a bunch of white Cornell kids in a private little world where we competed fiercely (but only with one another—no one else mattered!) for grades and test scores and solutions to brain teasers. We were the sort of kids other kids hated: the ones who would run around compiling lists of everyone else's test scores and would badger guidance counselors into admitting their errors in arithmetic (no computers then) in order to raise our class ranks a few notches. I held my own in this bunch, although I was forced by the norms of the fac-brat community to retake the Mathematics Level II achievement test to raise a humiliating score of 780 to an acceptable 800. (No one had yet told me that standardized tests were culturally biased against me.) Like the rest of the fac-brats, I yearned for the sobriquet "brilliant," and tried desperately to convince myself and everyone else who would listen that I had the grades and test scores to deserve it.

And yet there were unnerving indications that others did not see me as just another fac-brat, that they saw me instead as that black kid who hung out with the Cornell kids. There was, for example, the recruiter from Harvard College who asked to see those he considered the brightest kids in the school; I was included, so a guidance counselor said, because I was black. And when I decided that I wanted to attend Stanford University, I was told by a teacher that I would surely be admitted because I was black and I was smart. Not because I was smart and not even because I was smart and black, but because I was black and smart: the skin color always preceding any other observation.

Achievement instead of merit

All of this came to a head at National Merit Scholarship time. In those days (this was the early 1970s), the National Merit Scholarship Qualifying Test was a separate examination, not combined with the Preliminary Scholastic Aptitude Test as it later would be. When the qualifying scores came in, I was in heaven. Mine was the third highest in the school. I saw my future then—best fac-brat!—and awaited my National Merit Scholarship. Instead, I won a National Achievement Scholarship, presented, in the awkward usage of the day, to "outstanding Negro students." Well, all right. If one wants more black students to go to college, one had better provide the necessary resources. College is expensive and money is money. Still, at first I was insulted; I saw my "best fac-brat" status slipping away, for what I craved was a National *Merit* Scholarship, the one not for the best black students, but for the *best* students. So I was turned down.

Here it is useful to add some perspective. All through my adolescence, when I failed at some intellectual task (always measuring failure by my distance from the top), I usually, and properly, blamed myself. At times, however, I attributed my inability to reach my goals as a kind of conspiracy to keep me, a black kid, from reaping the rewards I imagined my achievements deserved, and, at times, to keep me from even trying. And sometimes the conspiracy was real.

Particularly vivid is my memory of moving from a mostly black elementary school to a mostly white junior high school, where I was not allowed to enroll in even a basic Spanish class, despite three years' study of the language, because, my mother was told, the limited spaces were all allocated to graduates of a particular elementary school—which happened to be all white. I was assigned to vocational education instead. And when I moved on to high school, carrying with me an A average in mathematics and excellent test scores, not only was I prevented from enrolling in the highest math section—I was not even told that it existed!

Having faced these barriers before, I readily assumed that the National Achievement program was another. (In fact, for nearly twenty years, my memory of the incident was that I was forced to choose between accepting a National Achievement Scholarship and remaining eligible for a National Merit Scholarship.) But when the National Merit people reassured me that I could accept one and remain eligible for the other, I accepted the offered scholarship, and even competed for the cherished National Merit Scholarship—which I didn't get. (That year, like most years, some students won both.) In time, I would come to support racially targeted scholarship programs. As a nervous 17-year-old, however, I worried that such programs were examples of the same old lesson: the smartest students of color were not considered as capable as the smartest white students, and therefore would not be allowed to compete with them, but only with one another.

The "best black" syndrome

I call it the "best black" syndrome, and all black people who have done well in school are familiar with it. We are measured by a different yardstick: *first black, only black, best black.* The best black syndrome is cut from the same cloth as the implicit and demeaning tokenism that often accompanies racial preferences: "Oh, we'll tolerate so-and-so at our hospital or in our firm or on our faculty, because she's the best black." Not because she's the best-qualified candidate, but because she's the best-qualified *black* candidate. She can fill the black slot. And then the rest of the slots can be filled in the usual way: with the best-*qualified* candidates.

This dichotomy between "best" and "best black" is not merely something manufactured by racists to denigrate the abilities of professionals who are not white. On the contrary, the durable and demeaning stereotype of black people as unable to compete with white ones is reinforced by advocates of certain forms of affirmative action. It is reinforced, for example, every time employers are urged to set aside test scores (even, in some cases, on tests that are good predictors of job performance) and to hire from separate lists, one of the best white scorers, the other of the best black ones. It is reinforced every time state pension plans are pressed to invest some of their funds with "minority-controlled" money management firms, even if it turns out that the competing "white" firms have superior track records.[1] It is reinforced every time students demand that universities commit to hiring some pre-set number of minority faculty members. What all of these people are really saying is, "There are black folks out there. Go and find the best of them." And the best black syndrome is further reinforced, almost unthinkingly, by politicians or bureaucrats or faculty members who see these demands as nothing more than claims for simple justice.

Diversity vs. quality

Successful black students and professionals have repeatedly disproved the proposition that the best black minds are not as good as the best white ones, but the stereotype lingers, even among the most ardent friends of civil rights. In my own area of endeavor, academia, I hear this all the time from people who should know better. It is not at all unusual for white professors, with no thought that they are indulging a demeaning stereotype, to argue for hiring the best available professors of color, whether or not the individuals on whom that double-edged mantle is bestowed meet the usual appointment standards. I put aside for the moment the question of the fairness of the standards, for the white people I am describing have few doubts about *that*; I have in mind white people who argue with straight faces for the hiring of black people *they themselves* do not believe are good enough to be hired without extra points for race. For example, one prominent law professor, a strong and sincere proponent of racial diversity, sent me a list of scholars in his field who might be considered for appointment to the Yale faculty. The first part of the list set out the names of the best people in the field; the second part, the names of people who were so-so; and the last part, the names of the leading "minorities and women" in the field, none of whom apparently qualified (in his judgment) for even the "so-so" category, let alone the best. I know that my colleague acted with the best of intentions, but the implicit invitation offered by this extraordinary document was to choose between diversity and quality. I suspect that to this day he is unaware of any insult and actually believes he was advancing the cause of racial justice.

"No responsible advocate of affirmative action," argues Ira Glasser, "opposes merit or argues . . . that standards should be reduced in order to meet affirmative action goals."[2] Perhaps not; but the language of standards and merit is slippery at best. I am reminded of a conversation I had some years ago with a veteran civil rights litigator who, concerned at charges that affirmative action sometimes results in hiring unqualified candidates, drew a sharp distinction between *unqualified* and *less qualified*. An employer, he mused, does not have to hire the *best* person for the job, as long as everyone hired is *good enough* to do the job. Consequently, he reasoned, it is perfectly fine to require employers to hire black applicants who are less qualified than some white applicants, as long as the black candidates are capable of doing the job. A tidy argument in its way, but, of course, another example of an almost unconscious acceptance of a situation in which an employer is made to distinguish between the best black candidates and the best ones.

I have had trouble escaping an assumption [underlying] the worst forms of affirmative action: that black people cannot compete intellectually with white people.

Even our sensible but sometimes overzealous insistence that the rest of the nation respect the achievements of black culture might reinforce the depressing dichotomy: if we insist, as often we must, that others appreciate "our" music and "our" literature, we should not be surprised if those others come to think of the best of our music and the best of our literature as distinct from the best music and the best literature. Indeed, this is the implication of Stanley Crouch's vigorous argument (on which I here express no view) that white critics accept a level of mediocrity from black artists, filmmakers, and writers that they would never tolerate from creative people who are white.[3]

I was told by a teacher that I would surely be admitted [to Stanford University] because I was black and I was smart. Not because I was smart.

The best black syndrome creates in those of us who have benefited from racial preferences a peculiar contradiction. We are told over and over that we are among the best black people in our professions. And in part we are flattered, or should be, because, after all, those who call us the best black lawyers or doctors or investment bankers consider it a compliment. But to professionals who have worked hard to succeed, flattery of this kind carries an unsubtle insult, for we yearn to be called what our achievements often deserve: simply the best—no qualifiers needed! In *this* society, however, we sooner or later must accept that being viewed as the best blacks is part of what has led us to where we are; and we must further accept that to some of our colleagues, black as well as white, we will never be anything else.

The rewards of being the "best black"

Despite these rather unsettling pitfalls, many of us resist the best black syndrome less than we should, and one of the reasons is surely that it can bestow considerable benefits. Racial preferences are perhaps the most obvious benefit, but there are others. In high school, for example, I quickly stood out, if only because I was the lone black student in any number of honors and advanced placement courses. Perhaps my intellect was not unusually keen; although I did as well as anyone, I have always thought that with proper training, scoring well on standardized tests is no great trick. Nevertheless, other students and, eventually, teachers as well concluded that I was particularly sharp. These perceptions naturally fed my ego, because all I really wanted from high school was to be considered one of the best and brightest.

What I could not see then, but see clearly now, two decades later, is that while the perceptions others had of my abilities were influenced in part by grades and test scores, they were further influenced by the fact that students and teachers (black and white alike) were unaccustomed to the idea that a black kid could sit among the white kids as an equal, doing as well, learning as much, speaking as ably, arguing with as much force. In their experience, I was so different that I had to be exceptional. But exceptional in a specific and limited sense: the best black.

College was not much different. My college grades were somewhat better than average, but at Stanford in the era of grade inflation, good grades were the norm. Nevertheless, I quickly discovered that black students with good grades stood out from the crowd. Other students and many of my professors treated me as a member of some odd and fascinating species. I sat among them as an equal in seminars, my papers were as good as anyone else's, so I had to be exceptionally bright. In their experience, it seemed, no merely ordinarily smart black person could possibly sit among them as an equal.

In law school, the trend continued. I was fortunate enough to come early to the attention of my professors, but all I was doing was playing by the rules: talking in class with reasonable intelligence, exhibiting genuine interest in questions at the podium later, and treating papers and examinations as matters of serious scholarship rather than obstacles to be overcome. Lots of students did the same—but, in the stereotyped visions of some of my professors, not lots of black students. Here was the best black syndrome at work once more: I was not just another bright student with an enthusiastic but untrained intellect; I was a bright *black* student, a fact that apparently made a special impression.

A lingering stereotype

The stultifying mythology of racism holds that black people are intellectually inferior. Consistent survey data over the years indicate that this stereotype persists.[4] Such incidents as those I have described, however, make me somewhat skeptical of the familiar complaint that because of this mythology, black people of intellectual talent have a harder time than others in proving their worth. My own experience suggests quite the contrary, that like a flower blooming in winter, intellect is more readily noticed where it is not expected to be found. Or, as a black investment banker has put the point, "Our mistakes are amplified, but so are our successes."[5] And it is the amplification of success that makes the achieving black student or professional into the best black.

When people assign to a smart black person the status of best black, they do so with the purest of motives: the curing of bewilderment. There must be an explanation, the reasoning runs, and the explanation must be that this black person, in order to do as well as white people, is exceptionally bright. What I describe is not racism in the sense of a design to oppress, but it is in its racialist assumption of inferiority every bit as insulting and nearly as tragic. The awe and celebration with which our achievements are often greeted (by black and white people alike) suggest a widespread expectation that our achievements will be few. The surprise is greater, perhaps, when our achievements are intellectual, but other achievements, too, seem to astonish. The astonishment, moreover, takes a long time to fade: even, or perhaps especially, in the era of affirmative action, it seems, the need to prove one's professional worth over and over again has not receded.

Boxed in

Affirmative action, to be sure, did not create this particular box into which black people are routinely stuffed. Throughout the long, tragic history of the interaction between white people and people of color in America (it is too often forgotten that there were people of color here before there were white people), the society has treated white as normal and color as an aberration that must be explained or justified or apologized for. Black people have always been the target of openly racist assumptions, perhaps the worst among these being that we are a stupid, primitive people. Every intellectual attainment by black people in America has been greeted with widespread suspicion. When the American Missionary Association and other abolitionist groups established black colleges in the South after the Civil War and determined to offer to the freed slaves and their progeny classical educations (Eurocentric educations, I suppose they would be called on today's campuses), emulating those available at the best Northern schools, editorialists had a field day. By the turn of the century, a standing joke had it that when two black students met on the campus of one of these colleges, the first greeted the second with, "Is yo' done yo' Greek yet?" The joke has faded from national memory, but its import, I fear, remains part of the nation's swirling racial consciousness.

Small wonder, then, that every black professional, in our racially conscious times, is assumed to have earned his or her position not by being among the best available but by being among the best available blacks. Any delusions to the contrary I might have harbored about my own achievements were shattered a few months after I was voted tenure at the Yale Law School. Late one night, a reporter for the campus newspaper called my home to say that the paper was doing a story about my promotion. Why was that? I wanted to know. Lots of law professors earn tenure, I said. Oh, I know, said the reporter, unabashed. Still, wasn't it true that I was the first black one? But that was the luck of the draw, I protested. It could as easily have been someone else. And besides, I wanted to shout, but dared not; besides, that isn't why I was promoted! (I hope.)

The durable and demeaning stereotype of black people as unable to compete with white ones is reinforced by advocates of certain forms of affirmative action.

My protests mattered not a jot, and the newspaper ran its story. A banner headline on the front page screamed that the law faculty had, for the first time, voted to promote a black professor to tenure. The tone of the article—years of lily-whiteness in the academy was its theme—suggested that my promotion was simple justice. But justice of a special sort: not the justice of earned reward for a job well done, but the justice due me as a professor who happens to be black. Whether I was a strong scholar or a weak one, a creative thinker or a derivative one, a diligent researcher or a lazy one, a good teacher or a bad one, mattered less to the newspaper than the fact that I was a black one. Evidently I had finally arrived, had I but the gumption to acknowledge it, as one of the best blacks.

Oppressed by affirmative action

I muted my protest, however. I did not complain, to the newspaper or to others, that I felt oppressed by this vision of tenure as an extension of affirmative action. Like many other black professionals, I simply wanted to be left alone to do my work. My hope, then as now, was that if I earned a place in the academic world, it would be for the seriousness of my research and the thoughtful contributions I hoped to make to legal knowledge—not for the color of my skin. Most of the scholarship I have committed has related to the separation of powers in the federal government, the regulation of intellectual property,[6] and the relationship of law and religion—to the lay person, perhaps not the most thrilling of topics, but, for me, intellectually engaging and lots of fun. I have always relished the look of surprise in the eyes of people who, having read my work in these areas, meet me for the first time. My favorite response (this really did happen) came at an academic conference at the University of Michigan Law School, where a dapper, buttoned-down young white man glanced at my name tag, evidently ignored the name but noted the school, and said, "If you're at Yale, you must know this Carter fellow who wrote that article about thus-and-so." Well, yes, I admitted. I did know that Carter fellow slightly. An awkward pause ensued. And then the young man, realizing his error, apologized with a smile warm enough to freeze butter.

The awe and celebration with which our achievements are often greeted . . . suggest a widespread expectation that our achievements will be few.

"Oh," he said, *"you're* Carter." (I have since wondered from time to time whether, had I been white and the error a less telling one, his voice would have been inflected differently: "You're *Carter."* Think about it.) Naturally, we then discussed the article, which happened to be about the separation of powers, and by way of showing the sincerity of his apology, he gushed about its quality in terms so adulatory that a casual observer might have been excused for thinking me the second coming of Oliver Wendell Holmes or, more likely, for thinking my interlocutor an idiot. (That gushing is part of the peculiar relationship between black intellectuals and the white ones who seem loath to criticize us for fear of being branded racists—which is itself a mark of racism of a sort.) I suppose I should have been flattered, although, if the truth is told, I quickly gained the impression that he was excited more by the political uses to which my argument might be put than by the analysis in the article itself.

But there it was! The Best Black Syndrome! It had, as they say, stood up and bitten me! Since this young man liked the article, its author could not, in his initial evaluation, have been a person of color. He had not even conceived of that possibility, or he would have glanced twice at my name tag. No, if the work was of high quality, the author had to be white—there was no room for doubt! The best blacks don't do this stuff!

And if you're black, you can't escape it! It's everywhere, this awkward set of expectations. No matter what you might accomplish (or imagine yourself to have accomplished), the label follows you. A friend of mine who works in the financial services field—I'll call him X—tells the story of his arrival at a client's headquarters. The client had been told that a supervisor was on the way to straighten out a particularly knotty problem. When my friend arrived, alone, and gave his name, the client said, "But where is the supervisor? Where is Mr. X?" With my friend standing right in front of him, name already announced! My friend, being black, could not possibly be the problem solver who was awaited. He was only . . . THE BEST BLACK! The winner of the coveted prize!

And that's the way it works. This is the risk some critics see in setting up Afro-American Studies departments: Isn't there a good chance that the school will dismiss the professors in the department as simply the best blacks, saying, in effect, don't worry about the academic standards the rest of us have to meet, you've got your own department? The answer is yes, of course, the school might do that—but that isn't an argument against Afro-American studies as a discipline, any more than it's an argument against hiring black faculty at all. It's just an admission that this is the way many of the white people who provide affirmative action programs and other goodies tend to think about them: there's Category A for the smart folks, and Category B for the best blacks. It's also a reminder to all people of color that our parents' advice was true: we really do have to work twice as hard to be considered half as good.

The need to adapt

This is an important point for those who are trapped by the best black syndrome. We cannot afford, ever, to let our standards slip. There are too many doubters waiting in the wings to pop out at the worst possible moment and cry, "See? Told you!" The only way to keep them off the stage is to make our own performances so good that there is no reasonable possibility of calling them into question. It isn't fair that so much should be demanded of us, but what has life to do with fairness? It was the artist Paul Klee, I believe, who said that one must adapt oneself to the contents of the paintbox. This is particularly true for upwardly mobile professionals who happen to be people of color, for people of color have had very little say about what those contents are.

So we have to adapt ourselves, a point I finally came to accept when I was in law school. In those days, the black students spent lots of time sitting around and discussing our obligations, if any, to the race. (I suppose black students still sit around and hold the same conversation.) In the course of one such conversation over a casual lunch, I blurted out to a classmate my driving ambition. It infuriated me, I said, that no matter what we might accomplish, none of us could aspire to anything more than the role of best black. What we should do for the race, I said, was achieve. Shatter stereotypes. Make white doubters think twice about our supposed intellectual inferiority.

A few years later, I foolishly imagined that I had attained my goal. It was the fall of 1981, and I was a young lawyer seeking a teaching position at a law school. I had, I was certain, played my cards right. In my law school years, I had managed to get to know a professor or two, and some of them liked me. I had compiled the right paper record before setting out to hunt for a job: my résumé included practice with a well-regarded law firm, good law school grades, service on the *Yale Law Journal*, and a spate of other awards and honors, including a clerkship with a Justice of the Supreme Court of the United States. One might have thought, and I suppose I thought it myself, that someone with my credentials would have no trouble landing a teaching job. But what people told me was that any school would be happy to have a black professor with my credentials. (Did a white professor need more, or did white professors just make their schools unhappy?) In the end, I was fortunate enough to collect a flattering set of job offers, but the taste was soured for me, at least a little, by the knowledge that whatever my qualifications, they probably looked more impressive on the résumé of someone black.

Affirmative action obscures achievement

There is an important point here, one that is missed by the critics who point out (correctly, I think) that affirmative action programs tend to call into question the legitimate achievements of highly qualified black professionals. Yes, they do; but that is not the end of the story. A few years ago, in a panel discussion on racial preferences, the economist Glenn Loury noted that the Harvard Law School had on its faculty two black professors who are also former law clerks for Justices of the Supreme Court of the United States. (As I write [1991], I believe that the number is three.) It isn't fair, he argued, that they should be dismissed as affirmative action appointments when they are obviously strongly qualified for the positions they hold. He is right that it isn't fair to dismiss them and he is right that they are obviously qualified, but it is also true that there are nowadays literally dozens of similarly qualified candidates for teaching positions every year. It is no diminution of the achievements of the professors Loury had in mind to point out that there is no real way to tell whether they would have risen to the top if not for the fact that faculties are on the lookout for highly qualified people of color. The same is surely true for many black people rising to the top of political, economic, and educational institutions.

There is a distinction here, however, that even the harshest critics of affirmative action should be willing to concede. Hiring to fill a slot that must be filled—the black slot, say—is not the same as using race to sort among a number of equally qualified candidates. Put otherwise, yes, it is true that the result of racial preferences is sometimes the hiring of black people not as well qualified as white people who are turned away, and preferences of that kind do much that is harmful and little that is good. But preferences can also be a means of selecting highly qualified black people from a pool of people who are all excellent. True, employers will almost always claim to be doing the second even when they are really doing the first; but that does not mean the second is impossible to do. And if an employer undertakes the second method, a sorting among the excellent, then although there might be legitimate grounds for concern, a criticism on the ground of lack of qualification of the person hired cannot be among them.

Struggling to be taken seriously

Ah, but are our analytical antennae sufficiently sensitive to detect the difference? I am not sure they are, and the sometimes tortured arguments advanced by the strongest advocates of affirmative action occasionally leave me with a bleak and hopeless sense that all people of color who are hired for the tasks for which their intellects and professional training have prepared them will be dismissed, always, as nothing more than the best blacks. And I draw from all of this two convictions: first, that affirmative action will not alter this perception; and, second, that white Americans will not change it simply because it is unjust. Consequently change, if change there is to be, is in *our* hands—and the only change for which we can reasonably hope will come about because we commit ourselves to battle for excellence, to show ourselves able to meet any standard, to pass any test that looms before us, in short, to form ourselves into a vanguard of black professionals who are simply too good to ignore.

And that, I suppose, is why I relish the reactions of those who have liked my work without knowing I am black: in my mind, I am proving them wrong, as I promised I would at that lunch so many years ago. No doubt my pleasure at the widened eyes is childish, but it is sometimes a relief to be sure for once that it is really the work they like, not the-unexpected-quality-of-the-work-given-the-naturally-inferior-intellects-of-those-with-darker-skins. It is a commonplace of social science, a matter of common sense as well, that an observer's evaluation of a piece of work is frequently influenced by awareness of the race of the author. Happily, I have found that people who like my work before they learn that I am black do not seem to like it less once they discover my color.[7]

Every black professional . . . is assumed to have earned his or her position not by being among the best available but by being among the best available blacks.

And when those who read my work *do* know that I am black? Well, any prejudices that the readers might bring to bear are, at least, nothing new. John Hope Franklin, in his sparkling essay on "The Dilemma of the American Negro Scholar," details the struggles of black academics during the past century to have their work taken seriously by white scholars.[8] Although progress has obviously been made, the struggle Franklin describes is not yet ended, which means I have to face the likelihood that many white scholars who read my work will judge it by a different standard than the one they use to judge the work of white people. Perhaps the standard will be higher, perhaps the standard will be lower, perhaps the standard will simply involve different criteria—but whatever the standard, all I can do is try to carry out the instruction that black parents have given their children for generations, and make the work not simply as good as the work of white scholars of similar background, but better. Sometimes I succeed, sometimes I fail; but to be a professional is always to strive. And while I am perfectly willing to concede the unfairness of a world that judges black people and white people by different standards, I do not lose large amounts of sleep over it. A journalist friend recently told my wife and me that he is tired of hearing black people complain about having to work twice as hard as white people to reach the same level of success. He says that if that's what we have to do, that's what we have to do, and it would not be a bad thing at all for us as a race to develop that habit as our defining characteristic: "Oh, you know those black people, they always work twice as hard as everybody else." If you can't escape it, then make the most of it: in my friend's racial utopia, it would no longer be taken as an insult to be called by a white colleague the best black.

The "star system"

My desire to succeed in the professional world without the aid of preferential treatment is hardly a rejection of the unhappy truth that the most important factor retarding the progress of people of color historically has been society's racism. It is, rather, an insistence on the opportunity to do what some people said I would not be allowed to, what I promised at that fateful lunch I would: to show the world that we who are black are not so marked by our history of racist oppression that we are incapable of intellectual achievement on the same terms as anybody else.

In a society less marked by racist history, the intellectual achievements of people of color might be accepted as a matter of course. In *this* society, however, they are either ignored or applauded, but never accepted as a matter of course. As I have said, however, the general astonishment when our achievements are intellectual carries with it certain benefits. Perhaps chief among these is the possibility of entrée to what I call the "star system." The characteristics of the star system are familiar to anyone who has attended college or professional school or has struggled upward on the corporate ladder, and it has analogues in sports, the military, and other arenas. Early in their careers, a handful of individuals are marked by their teachers or supervisors as having the potential for special success, even greatness. Thereafter, the potential stars are closely watched. Not every person marked early as a possible star becomes one, but the vast majority of those who are never marked will never star. Even very talented individuals who lack entrée to the star system may never gain attention in the places that matter: the hushed and private conference rooms (I can testify to their existence, having sat in more than a few) where money is spent and hiring and promotion decisions are made.

Whether I was a strong scholar or a weak one . . . mattered less to the newspaper than the fact that I was a black one.

Getting into the star system is not easy, and the fact that few people of color scramble to the top of it should scarcely be surprising. The reason is not any failing in our native abilities—although it is true that only in the past decade have we been present as students in numbers sufficient to make entry more plausible—but the social dynamics of the star system itself. Entrée is not simply a matter of smarts, although that helps, or of working hard, although that helps, too. The star system rewards familiarity, comfort, and perseverance. It usually begins on campus, and so do its problems. One must get to know one's professors. Most college and professional school students are far too intimidated by their professors to feel comfortable getting to know them well, and for many students of color, already subject to a variety of discomforts, this barrier may seem especially high. When one feels uneasy about one's status in the classroom to begin with, the task of setting out to get to know the professor personally may seem close to insuperable. The fact that some students of color indeed reap the benefits of the star system does not alter the likelihood that many more would never dream of trying.

I relish the reactions of those who have liked my work without knowing I am black.

Exclusion from the star system is costly. Anyone left out will meet with difficulties in being taken seriously as a candidate for entry-level hiring at any of our most selective firms and institutions, which is why the failure of people of color to get into the star system makes a difference. Still, there is an opportunity here: because so little is expected of students of color, intellectual attainment is sometimes seen as a mark of genuine brilliance. (None of the merely ordinarily smart need apply!) So the best black syndrome can have a salutary side effect: it can help those trapped inside it get through the door of the star system. Certainly it worked that way for me. (Who *is* this character? my professors seemed to want to know.) The star system, in turn, got me in the door of the academy at the entry level. (From the doorway, I would like to think, I made the rest of the journey on my own; my achievements ought to speak for themselves. But in a world in which I have heard my colleagues use the very words *best black* in discussions of faculty hiring, I have no way to tell.) So, yes, I am a beneficiary of both the star system and the best black syndrome. Yet I hope it is clear that I am not a fan of either. The star system is exclusionary and incoherent; the best black syndrome is demeaning and oppressive. Both ought to be abandoned.

The glass ceiling

Consider the so-called glass ceiling, the asserted reluctance of corporations to promote people of color to top management positions. If indeed the glass ceiling exists, it is very likely a function of the star system. If people of color tend to have trouble getting in good, as the saying goes, with their professors, they are likely to have as much or more trouble getting in good with their employers. And if, once hired, people who are not white face difficulties in finding mentors, powerful institutional figures to smooth their paths, then they will naturally advance more slowly. Oh, there will always be some black participants in the star system, not as tokens but as people who have, as I said, taken to heart the adage that they must be twice as good. (One need but think of Colin Powell [former Chairman, Joint Chiefs of Staff] or William Coleman [U.S. secretary of transportation from 1975–1977 and second African American cabinet member in U.S. history].) Still, plenty of people of color who are merely as good as or slightly better than white people who are inside the star system will find themselves outside. The social turns do not work for them, and their advancement on the corporate ladder will be slow or nonexistent.

To be sure, the star system cannot get all of the blame for the dearth of people who are not white in (and, especially, at the top of) the professions. That there is present-day racism, overt and covert, might almost go without saying, except that so many people keep insisting there isn't any. But one should not assume too readily that contemporary discrimination explains all of the observed difference. Groups are complex and no two groups are the same. With cultural and other differences, it would be surprising if all group outcomes were identical. When the nation's odious history of racial oppression is grafted onto any other differences that might exist, the numbers are less surprising still. What would be surprising would be if we as a people had so successfully shrugged off the shackles of that history as to have reached, at this relatively early stage in the nation's evolution, economic and educational parity.

But the star system is not exactly blameless, either. Any system that rewards friendship and comfort rather than merit will burden most heavily those least likely to find the right friends.[9] It is ironic, even awkward, to make this point in an era when the attack on meritocracy is so sharply focused, but the claims pressed by today's critics in that attack—bigotry, unconscious bias, corrupt and malleable standards, social and cultural exclusion—are among the reasons that led other ethnic groups in the past to insist on the establishment of measurable systems for rewarding merit. The star system is a corrupt and biased means for circumventing the meritocratic ideal, but its corruption should not be attributed to the ideal itself.

Searching for quality

None of this means that affirmative action is the right answer to the difficulties the star system has spawned. Among the group of intellectuals known loosely (and, I believe, often inaccurately) as black conservatives, there is a widely shared view that the removal of artificial barriers to entry into a labor market is the proper goal to be pursued by those who want to increase minority representation. The economist Walter Williams often cites the example of cities like New York that limit the number of individuals permitted to drive taxicabs. No wonder, he says, there are so few black cabdrivers: it's too difficult to get into the market. Consequently, says Williams, New York should abolish its limits and, subject only to some basic regulatory needs, open the field to anyone. This, he says, would automatically result in an increase in black drivers—assuming, that is, that there are black people who want to drive cabs.

People of color do not need special treatment in order to advance in the professional world.

Other strategies, too, are easy to defend. For example, it is difficult to quarrel with the idea that an employer concerned about diversity—whatever its needs and hiring standards—should be as certain as possible that any candidate search it conducts is designed to yield the names of people of color who fit the search profile. After centuries of exclusion by design, it would be a terrible tragedy were black and other minority professionals excluded through inadvertence. Mari Matsuda has argued that a serious intellectual ought to make an effort to read books by members of groups not a part of his or her familiar experience, and I think she is quite right.[10] It is in the process of that determined reading—that searching—that the people who have been overlooked will, if truly excellent, eventually come to light.

The example can be generalized. Searching is the only way to find outstanding people of color, which is why all professional employers should practice it. Although the cost of a search is not trivial, the potential return in diversity, without any concomitant lowering of standards, is enormous—provided always that the employer is careful to use the search only to turn up candidates, not as a means of bringing racial preferences into the hiring process through the back door. For it is easy, but demeaning, to conflate the goal of searching with the goal of hiring, and to imagine therefore that the reason for the search is to ensure that the optimal number of black people are hired. It isn't. The reason for the search is to find the blacks among the best, not the best among the blacks.

No guarantees

If this distinction is borne firmly in mind, then an obligation to search will of course provide no guarantee that the statistics will improve. But I am not sure that a guarantee is what we should be seeking. People of color do not need special treatment in order to advance in the professional world; we do not need to be considered the best blacks, competing only with one another for the black slots. On the contrary, our goal ought to be to prove that we can compete with anybody, to demonstrate that the so-called pool problem, the alleged dearth of qualified entry-level candidates who are not white, is at least partly a myth. So if we can gain for ourselves a fair and equal chance to show what we can do—what the affirmative action literature likes to call a level playing field—then it is something of an insult to our intellectual capacities to insist on more.

And of course, although we do not like to discuss it, the insistence on more carries with it certain risks. After all, an employer can hire a candidate because the employer thinks that person is the best one available or for some other reason: pleasing a powerful customer, rewarding an old friend, keeping peace in the family, keeping the work force all white, getting the best black. When the employer hires on one of these other grounds, it should come as no surprise if the employee does not perform as well as the best available candidate would have. There will be times when the performance will be every bit as good, but those will not be the norm unless the employer is a poor judge of talent; and if the employer consistently judges talent poorly, a second, shrewder judge of talent will eventually put the first employer out of business.[11] That is not, I think, a web in which we as a people should want to be entangled.

Racial preferences are the wrong answer

Racial preferences, in sum, are not the most constructive method for overcoming the barriers that keep people of color out of high-prestige positions. They are often implemented in ways that are insulting, and besides, they can carry considerable costs. Although there are fewer unfair and arbitrary barriers to the hiring and retention of black professionals than there once were, many barriers remain, and the star system, although some few of us benefit from it, is prominent among them. But if the barriers are the problem, then it is the barriers themselves that should be attacked. Should the star system be brushed aside, our opportunities would be considerably enhanced because many of the special advantages from which we are excluded would vanish.

Racial preferences are founded on the proposition that the achievements of their beneficiaries would be fewer if the preferences did not exist.

Getting rid of the star system will not be easy. I have discovered through painful experience that many of its most earnest white defenders—as well as many of those who pay lip service to overturning it but meanwhile continue to exploit it—are also among the most ardent advocates of hiring black people who, if white, they would consider second-rate. They are saying, in effect, We have one corrupt system for helping out our friends, and we'll be happy to let you have one for getting the numbers right. Faced with such obduracy, small wonder that racial preferences seem an attractive alternative.

But people of color must resist the urge to join the race to the bottom. The stakes are too high. I am sensitive to Cornell University Professor Isaac Kramnick's comment that even if a school hires some black professors who are not first-rate, "it will take till eternity for the number of second-rate blacks in the university to match the number of second-rate whites."[12] Point taken: one can hardly claim that elite educational institutions have been perfect meritocracies. However, the claim that there are incompetent whites and therefore incompetent blacks should be given a chance is unlikely to resonate with many people's visions of justice. Because of the racial stereotyping that is rampant in our society, moreover, any inadequacies among second-rate white professionals are unlikely to be attributed by those with the power to do something about it to whites as a whole; with black professionals, matters are quite unfairly the other way around, which is why the hiring of second-rate black professionals in any field would be detrimental to the effort to break down barriers.

Excellence, not adequacy

The corruption of the meritocratic ideal with bias and favoritism offers professionals who are not white an opportunity we should not ignore: the chance to teach the corrupters their own values by making our goal excellence rather than adequacy. Consider this perceptive advice to the black scholar from John Hope Franklin, one of the nation's preeminent historians: "He should know that by maintaining the highest standards of scholarship he not only becomes worthy but also sets an example that many of his contemporaries who claim to be the arbiters in the field do not themselves follow."[13] The need to beat down the star system should spur us not to demand more affirmative action but to exceed the achievements of those who manipulate the system to their advantage.

Besides, the star system does not taint every institution to an equal degree. Some hiring and promotion processes actually make sense. If we rush to graft systems of racial preference onto hiring processes rationally designed to produce the best doctors or lawyers or investment bankers or professors, we might all hope that the professionals hired because of the preferences turn out to be as good as those hired because they are expected to be the best, but no one should be surprised if this hope turns to ashes. Painful though this possibility may seem, it is consistent with a point that many supporters of affirmative action tend to miss, or at least to obscure: racial preferences that make no difference are unimportant.

Racial preferences are founded on the proposition that the achievements of their beneficiaries would be fewer if the preferences did not exist. Supporters of preferences cite a whole catalogue of explanations for the inability of people of color to get along without them: institutional racism, inferior education, overt prejudice, the lingering effects of slavery and oppression, cultural bias in the criteria for admission and employment. All of these arguments are most sincerely pressed, and some of them are true. But like the best black syndrome, they all entail the assumption that people of color cannot at present compete on the same playing field with people who are white. I don't believe this for an instant.

Notes

1. See, for example, the account of the debate in Maryland in *Bond Buyer*, 31 July 1990, p. 32.

2. Ira Glasser, "Affirmative Action and the Legacy of Racial Injustice," in *Eliminating Racism: Profiles in Controversy*, ed. Phyllis A. Katz and Dalmas A. Taylor (New York: Plenum Press, 1988), pp. 341, 350.

3. Stanley Crouch, *Notes of a Hanging Judge* (New York: Oxford University Press, 1990).

4. The most recent General Social Survey, a regular report of the widely respected National Opinion Research Center, found that 53 percent of white respondents consider black people generally less intelligent than white people. ("Whites Retain Negative View of Minorities, a Survey Finds," *New York Times*, 10 January 1991, p. B10.) Prior surveys through the late 1960s had shown a decline in the percentage of white respondents who consider black people less intelligent. Historical polling results on the attitudes of white Americans about black Americans are collected in National Research Council, *A Common Destiny: Blacks and American Society* (Washington, D.C.: National Academy Press, 1989), pp. 120–23. For a more detailed discussion of data collected during the 1980s, see Lee Sigelman and Susan Welch, *Black Americans' Views of Racial Inequality* (Cambridge: Cambridge University Press, 1991), esp. pp. 85–100.

5. Quoted in Colin Leinster, "Black Executives: How They're Doing," *Fortune*, 18 January 1988, p. 109.

6. Intellectual property is the field of law governing rights in intangible creations of the mind and includes such subjects as patents, copyrights, and trademarks.

7. Often, however, they do suddenly assume that I must possess a special expertise in the most sophisticated quandaries and delicately nuanced esoterica of civil rights law, areas that take years of careful study to master, no matter the contrary impression given by the sometimes simpleminded reporting on civil rights law in the mass media.

8. John Hope Franklin, "The Dilemma of the American Negro Scholar," in *Race and History: Selected Essays 1938–1988* (Baton Rouge: Louisiana State University Press, 1989), p. 295. The essay was originally published in 1963.

9. My description of the star system might usefully be compared to the French sociologist Pierre Bourdieu's analysis of the role of "cultural capital" and "social capital" in the maintenance of the class structure: Pierre Bourdieu, "Cultural Reproduction and Social Reproduction," in *Power and Ideology in Education*, ed. J. Karabel and A. H. Halsey (New York: Oxford University Press, 1977), p. 487. I am less sure than Bourdieu is that the system works principally to the benefit of the children of those already part of it; my concern with the star system is that it is exclusionary and at the same time a distortion of the meritocratic ideal.

10. Mari Matsuda, "Affirmative Action and Legal Knowledge: Planting Seeds in Plowed-up Ground," *Harvard Women's Law Journal* 11 (Spring 1988): 5–6.

11. Although it is sometimes said that racial discrimination serves the interests of capitalism, the inefficiency of prejudice in the market is well understood in economics. The classic analysis of the market costs of discrimination on the basis of race is Gary S. Becker, *The Economics of Discrimination* (Chicago: University of Chicago Press, 1957). Much of the analysis in Becker's book is mathematical and may be inaccessible to the lay reader. A recent and more accessible treatment of the same issue is Thomas Sowell, *Preferential Policies: An International Perspective* (New York: William Morrow, 1990), esp. pp. 20–40. For a discussion of the way that racial discrimination following the Civil War retarded the growth of the Southern economy, see Roger L. Ransom and Richard Sutch, *One Kind of Freedom: The Economic Consequences of Emancipation* (Cambridge: Cambridge University Press, 1977).

12. Quoted in Adam Begley, "Black Studies' New Era: Henry Louis Gates Jr.," *New York Times Magazine*, 1 April 1990, p. 24.

13. Franklin, "The Dilemma of the American Negro Scholar," p. 305.

6

Women Do Not Need Affirmative Action

Laura A. Ingraham

Laura A. Ingraham is a lawyer and news commentator based in Washington, D.C. She has served as law clerk to Supreme Court justice Clarence Thomas and is a member of Senator Robert Dole's Affirmative Action Working Group. Ingraham also serves on the advisory board of the Independent Women's Forum, a public-policy organization that advocates free market principles and individual rights.

Equal *opportunity*, the main objective of early feminists, does not mean guaranteeing women a certain number of slots at each rung upon the management ladder. Legislating equality of *results*—or quotas—unfairly rigs the competition for jobs, government contracts, and school admissions. Furthermore, it compromises women's credibility by denying them the chance to succeed without artificial aids. While affirmative action was instrumental in opening doors long closed to women, the programs have outlived their need. Those who argue for the continuation of gender-based group preferences ignore the tremendous successes women have achieved and incorrectly blame sexism where successes are not evident. These protesters do not speak for all women, many of whom look forward to proceeding with their careers fueled by their own power and nothing more.

Editor's Note: The following viewpoint was delivered as testimony before the House of Representatives Subcommittee on the Constitution during its April 3, 1995, hearing on "Group Preferences and the Law."

Preferential group treatment, whether mandated, encouraged, or even tolerated by the federal government, raises serious questions about a principle central to the American spirit—fairness. Thirty years after President John F. Kennedy's Executive Order 11246, in which he first espoused the concept of "affirmative action," we as a nation committed to equal opportunity must ask ourselves whether we have veered off course.

Laura A. Ingraham, testimony given before the U.S. House of Representatives Committee on the Judiciary, Subcommittee on the Constitution, April 3, 1995.

Merit is gender- and race-neutral

I first began thinking about the idea of gender preferences in 1980 as a high school student, when I heard then–presidential candidate Ronald Reagan, in whose Administration I would later work, promise that if elected he would nominate the first woman to sit on the Supreme Court. This somehow seemed wrong to me. I certainly believed a woman would make a good Justice, but I also thought people were supposed to be judged without regard to race or gender. A decade or so later, as a law clerk at the Supreme Court, I grew to respect Justice Sandra Day O'Connor personally and professionally—not because she was the first female Justice, but because she was a talented and dedicated Justice.

This coming Sunday [April 9, 1995] some women will descend on Washington to protest what the National Organization for Women calls recent "tyrannical measures" against women—such as the national groundswell for dismantling federal affirmative action programs. Rally organizers hope to persuade a public increasingly skeptical of group preferences that affirmative action is as crucial to the success of women in the workplace as it is for minorities. The tone of the press release announcing this rally resonates a siege-mentality, where women are being targeted for discrimination by men at every turn. Yet the literature makes no mention of the enormous gains that women have made.

Although we do not believe the majority of women in the United States share this pessimism, we are very concerned that if the federal government continues to countenance decisionmaking on the basis of gender, women will be relegated to a permanent second-class status, where they are not held to the same standards as their male counterparts, and therefore cannot compete on the merits for jobs, education, or promotions. Of course, we recognize that affirmative action did tremendous things for women, by opening previously closed doors in employment and education. With those doors now flung wide open, it is time to leave group preference, which was never intended to be a permanent solution, behind. Unfortunately, the array of federal programs that accord special treatment on the basis of gender have already created an unhealthy national climate. This gender trap creates animosity among men who are trying just as hard as their female counterparts to succeed and prosper, as well as among women who do not want people thinking they got where they are because of affirmative action.

The wrong yardstick

Whatever one wants to call it—group preferences, affirmative action, quotas or set-asides—what we have today in the form of federal policies and regulations is a system that has strayed far beyond what Presidents Kennedy or Lyndon B. Johnson initially understood affirmative action to mean. With the release of the U.S. Labor Department's Glass Ceiling Report the last week of March 1995, we see that well-educated and well-intentioned people measure women's progress not by whether they are being accorded equal opportunities to succeed—or fail—but by whether they are being proportionately represented in this or that management level or in a particular profession. Without statistical evidence of discriminatory actions or attitudes, the Commission attributed the fact that

only a small percentage of women occupied the highest positions in Fortune 500 companies to the "glass ceiling" phenomenon.

It is both simplistic and patronizing to conclude that women are con-
stantly thwarted by invisible barriers of silent sexism and discrimination,
and thus need government set-asides or preferences to make it in the
workforce. To many women, including those represented by the Independent Women's Forum, this mindset is as demeaning as it is flawed.
More significant, however, is the realization that tolerating gender preferences imperils the cause that true feminists originally championed—
equal *opportunity*. The goal of equal access to and advancement within the
workforce, which we all support, was never meant to be a guarantee that
women would constitute some fixed percentage of managerial positions
by the end of the century—or ever, for that matter.

---

*I certainly believed a woman would make a good
Justice, but I also thought people were supposed to be
judged without regard to race or gender.*

A careful reading of the Glass Ceiling Commission's own statistics suggests that in almost every segment of the working world, the combination
of equal opportunity and hard work have led to steady, impressive gains for
women. In 1992, women held 23 percent of corporate senior vice-president
positions versus 14 percent in 1982; the percentage of all female vice presidents more than doubled in the same period. From 1979 to 1993, women's
wages increased by a whopping 119 percent. Meanwhile, the percentage of
male managers fell from 65 percent to 51 percent. Yet according to affirmative action scholar Jonathan Leonard at the University of California,
none of these positive employment trends can be definitively traced to affirmative action. The Independent Women's Forum, and I think most
women, would cheer the conclusion that women's successes in the workplace are due not to social engineering, but to women's perseverance and
merit which they demonstrate when given a fair chance to compete.

Affirmative action grows obsolete

Oddly enough, some women seem to be having a hard time coming to
terms with the real progress women have made. Acknowledging the reality that women today have equal access to virtually every field and profession also means acknowledging the dilemma that often goes along
with these expanded choices—how to balance career and family. Is it not
possible that the relatively small percentage of women in senior-level
management positions in business is attributable to any number of reasons having nothing to do with discrimination, such as the fact that
women with children often choose to work fewer hours than their male
counterparts, or that working mothers find it more fulfilling to channel
their ambition into family rather than into work? These questions were
not even entertained in the Glass Ceiling Report.

It simply makes no sense to conclude that with women occupying
more than 40 percent of all managerial positions in American business,

not to mention comprising nearly half of the workforce and 51 percent of the population, our country's business leaders sit poised to displace women from top jobs as soon as federal affirmative action policies for women are abandoned. Certainly, if the federal government advocates and demands a merit-based approach to awarding grants or contracts or to hiring, women will fare just fine.

Of course discontinuing gender preferences does not and should not mean abandoning federal enforcement of anti-discrimination laws. Discriminatory practices should continue to be deterred and penalized through the appropriate statutory mechanisms. To brand those of us who want to see an end to preferential group treatment sexist or racist, which unfortunately many feminists continue to do, is demagoguery of the worst kind. Such scare tactics seem designed to accomplish one goal—to shut down debate about a critical issue. For a while those tactics worked. But as the fall elections of 1994 demonstrated, Americans are beginning to question previously unchallenged government presumptions. It is no longer taboo, for example, to argue that a municipality should not be deemed guilty of gender discrimination because it requires that all fire fighters be capable of carrying a 150-pound person from a burning building.

Earning one's achievements

Whether Congress decides to pass a law prohibiting preferential treatment based on gender and whether women support such a move will reveal much about both the way women are perceived and how they perceive themselves. Title VII of the 1964 Civil Rights Act provides: "Nothing contained in this title shall be interpreted to *require* [quotas or group preferences]." If we are going to be serious about ending group-based discrimination, Congress should amend that language to read that nothing in Title VII should be construed to *permit* gender, racial or other group preferences, quotas or set-asides.

By demanding real, not rigged, competition for jobs, promotions, or admission to academic institutions, women will be fulfilling the true goal of early feminists. By refusing to be judged by different criteria from men, whether for a police academy test or as a business seeking licensing rights from the Federal Communications Commission (FCC), women will erase any remaining doubts that they are up to the task. It will be refreshing when we stop hearing things like "She's a good *female* attorney," or "a bright *female* engineer," or an "experienced *female* pilot." When people have no cause to wonder whether a women was promoted or hired for any reason other than individual talent, women who succeed will be referred to as just plain *good*. I do not know any woman who would not rather succeed knowing she was the best person for the job, rather than wondering whether it was because of some goal, quota or timetable set by her employer.

7

Affirmative Action Should Be Eliminated

Arch Puddington

Arch Puddington writes frequently on American race relations and civil rights and is a senior scholar at Freedom House, a conservative research organization concerned with political and civil liberties.

Affirmative action is simply another name for racial preferences. As a policy, it affronts the most treasured American values—those of fairness and individualism. Most Americans oppose preference policies, which were prohibited—although the prohibitions were subsequently disregarded by political elites—in the original antidiscrimination legislation of the 1960s. Proponents claim that "institutional racism"—racism pervasive in America's social and economic institutions—justifies continued racial preferences. However, rather than achieve equality for minorities and women, the programs have spawned reverse discrimination, which has in turn caused increasing racial disharmony. Moreover, affirmative action has eroded academic and professional standards as schools and employers strive to meet mandated quotas. America's political leaders should eliminate all federal programs that extend racial preferences while retaining antidiscrimination laws for an America that truly offers equal opportunity.

The thinking behind the policy of racial preference which has been followed in America over the past quarter-century under the name of "affirmative action"[1] is best summed up by former Supreme Court Justice Harry Blackmun's famous dictum that, "In order to get beyond racism, we must first take race into account."

A contradiction in values

The Orwellian quality of Blackmun's admonition is obvious. Seldom has a democratic government's policy so completely contradicted the core values of its citizenry as racial preference does in violating the universally

Arch Puddington, "What to Do About Affirmative Action." Reprinted from *Commentary* (June 1995) by permission; all rights reserved.

held American ideals of fairness and individual rights, including the right to be free from discrimination. Not surprisingly, then, where Americans regarded the original civil-rights legislation as representing a long-over-due fulfillment of the country's democratic promise, they overwhelm-ingly see racial preference as an undemocratic and alien concept, a policy implemented by stealth and subterfuge and defended by duplicity and le-galistic tricks.

Seldom has a democratic government's policy so completely contradicted the core values of its citizenry as racial preference does.

Americans do not believe that past discrimination against blacks in the workplace justifies present discrimination against whites. Nor do they accept the thesis that tests and standards are tainted, *en masse*, by cultural bias against minorities. Having been taught in high-school civics classes that gerrymandering to ensure party domination represents a defect in democracy, Americans are bewildered by the argument that gerryman-dering is necessary to ensure the political representation of blacks and Hispanics. They are unimpressed by the contention that a university's ex-cellence is enhanced by the mere fact of racial and ethnic diversity in its student body, especially when entrance requirements must be lowered substantially to achieve that goal.

Americans, in short, oppose racial preference in all its embodiments, and have signified their opposition in opinion poll after opinion poll, usually by margins of three to one or more, with women as strongly op-posed as men, and with an impressive proportion of blacks indicating op-position as well. The contention, repeatedly advanced by advocates of preferential policies, that a national consensus exists in support of such policies has been true only at the level of political elites. Americans do support what might be called soft affirmative action, entailing special re-cruitment, training, and outreach efforts, and are willing to accept some short-term compensatory measures to rectify obvious cases of proven dis-crimination. But attitudes have, if anything, hardened against the kind of aggressive, numbers-driven preference schemes increasingly encountered in university admissions and civil-service hiring.

Refusing to let go

Nonetheless, up until this year [1995], racial preference in its various manifestations has been impressively resistant to calls for reform, much less elimination. In fact, race consciousness has begun to insinuate itself into areas which, common sense alone would suggest, should be immune to intrusive government social engineering. To cite but one example of this disturbing trend: Congress has mandated that guidelines be estab-lished guaranteeing the involvement of minorities (and women) in clini-cal research—a form of scientific experimentation by quota.

There is, furthermore, reason to question whether the advocates of race-conscious social policy continue to take seriously the objective of getting "beyond race," a condition which presumably would warrant the elimination of all preferential programs. The late Thurgood Marshall, an outspoken champion of preference while on the Supreme Court, is reported to have blurted out during an in-chambers discussion that blacks would need affirmative action for a hundred years. A similar opinion has been expressed by Benjamin Hooks, the former director of the National Association for the Advancement of Colored People (NAACP). Hooks contends that affirmative action in some form should be accepted as one of those permanent, irritating features of American life—he cited as examples speeding laws and the April 15 income-tax deadline—which citizens tolerate as essential to the efficient and just functioning of society.

Neither Marshall nor Hooks is regarded as an extremist on race matters; their advocacy of a permanent regime of affirmative action falls within the mainstream of present-day liberal thought. The promotion of "diversity"—the latest euphemism for preferential representation—is as fundamental to liberal governance as was the protection of labor unions in an earlier era. And until very recently, liberal proponents of preference clearly believed that history was on their side.

Thus, where enforcement agencies were formerly cautious in pressing affirmative action on the medical profession, the Clinton administration was formulating plans for a quota system throughout the health-care workforce. The goal, according to one memo of Hillary Clinton's task force, was nothing less than to ensure that this workforce achieve "sufficient racial, ethnic, gender, geographic, and cultural diversity to be representative of the people it serves." The task force also had plans to guide minority doctors into specialties while tracking other doctors into general practice. To realize this medical-care diversity blueprint, the task force proposed the creation of a bureaucracy with coercive powers to regulate the "geographic" and "cultural" distribution of physicians and other medical practitioners.

The entrance of quotas

How did America drift from the ideal of a color-blind society to the current environment of quotas, goals, timetables, race-norming, set-asides, diversity-training, and the like?

Those troubled by this question often refer wistfully to Martin Luther King, Jr.'s declaration that he hoped to see the day when his children would be judged by the content of their character and not by the color of their skin. Yet it must be recognized that even when King uttered those inspirational words at the 1963 March on Washington, they no longer reflected the thinking of crucial segments of the civil-rights movement. Already, increasingly influential black activists and their white supporters were advancing demands for hiring plans based on racial quotas. In pressing for such plans (then called compensatory treatment), the civil-rights movement was being joined by officials from the Kennedy administration, as well as by white intellectuals who, going further, announced that black economic equality could never be attained without a wholesale adjustment of standards and the merit principle.

These ruminations were not lost on the Dixiecrat opponents of desegregation, and the charge was soon made that Title VII of the pending civil-rights bill—the section dealing with discrimination in the work-place—would lead to the widespread practice of reverse discrimination. This in turn provoked a series of statements and speeches by stalwart liberals like Senators Hubert Humphrey, Joseph Clark, and Clifford Case, adamantly and unequivocally denying that the bill could be interpreted to permit racial preference.

In order to dispel lingering doubts, Humphrey and other supporters inserted an amendment to the bill declaring flatly that the law's purpose was to rectify cases of intentional discrimination and that it was not intended to impose sanctions simply because a workplace contained few blacks or because few blacks passed an employment test. Armed with this and similar clauses prohibiting reverse discrimination, Humphrey promised to "start eating the pages [of the civil-rights bill] one after another" if anyone could discover language in it "which provides that an employer will have to hire on the basis of percentage or quota."

The anti-preference language which had been added to ensure passage of the Civil Rights Act of 1964 was . . . not only ignored but treated as though it did not even exist.

Under normal circumstances, the insertion of unambiguous anti-preference language, combined with the condemnations of reverse discrimination by the bill's sponsors, would have been sufficient to prevent the subsequent distortion of the law's intent. But these protections turned out to be useless against the determination of the country's elites (in the political system, in the media, in the universities, and in the courts) to override them. Having concluded (especially after the urban riots of the late 60's) that social peace demanded racial preference, political leaders from both parties, along with a growing number of intellectuals and activists, both white and black, began looking upon the anti-preference clauses in Title VII as obstacles to be circumvented rather than guides to be followed. The anti-preference language which had been added to ensure passage of the Civil Rights Act of 1964 was now not only ignored but treated as though it did not even exist.

Hence there was no serious effort by either Congress or the courts or anyone else to rein in the civil-rights bureaucracy, which dismissed the anti-preference provisions with contempt from the very outset. A "big zero, a nothing, a nullity," is how these provisions were characterized by an official of the Equal Employment Opportunity Commission (EEOC) at the time. Federal enforcement officials in general, most of whom were white, were more aggressive in pursuing preferences, and less inclined to reflect on the broader implications of affirmative action, than were many mainstream black leaders of that day, some of whom—Roy Wilkins, Bayard Rustin, and Clarence Mitchell, for example—opposed reverse discrimination on moral and political grounds.

The part played by the EEOC in putting together the structure of racial preference cannot be overstated. In blithe and conscious disregard of the anti-preference sections of Title VII, EEOC officials broadened the definition of discrimination to encompass anything which contributed to unequal outcomes. In its most far-reaching move, the EEOC launched an all-out assault on employment testing. The agency's mindset was reflected in comments about "irrelevant and unreasonable standards," "the cult of credentialism," and "artificial barriers."

Yet despite the ingenuity of its lawyers in devising intricate arguments to circumvent the strictures against reverse discrimination—and despite the willingness of activist judges to accept these arguments—the EEOC could never have achieved its aims had it not been for a transformation of elite attitudes toward the problem of race in America.

"Institutional racism"

In 1964, the year the Civil Rights Act was passed, an optimistic and morally confident America believed that the challenge posed by the "Negro revolution" could be met through a combination of anti-discrimination laws, economic growth, and the voluntary good will of corporations, universities, and other institutions. But by the decade's end, a crucial segment of elite opinion had concluded that America was deeply flawed, even sick, and that racism, conscious or otherwise, permeated every institution and government policy. Where individual prejudice had previously been identified as the chief obstacle to black progress, now a new target, "institutional racism," was seen as the principal villain. And where it was once thought that democratic guarantees against discrimination, plus the inherent fairness of the American people, were sufficient to overcome injustice, the idea now took hold that since racism was built into the social order, coercive measures were required to root it out.

In this view, moreover, the gradualist Great Society [an agenda of social programs designed to fight poverty] approach launched by Lyndon Johnson, which stressed education, training, and the strengthening of black institutions, could not alleviate the misery of the inner-city poor, at least not as effectively as forcing employers to hire them. Even Johnson himself began calling for affirmative action and issued an executive order directing that federal contractors adopt hiring policies which did not discriminate on the basis of race (or gender); in a process that would soon became all too familiar, court decisions and the guidelines of regulators subsequently interpreted the directive as mandating racial balance in the workforce, thus paving the way for demands that companies doing business with the government institute what often amounted to quotas in order to qualify for contracts.

Little noticed at the time—or, for that matter, later—was that black America was in the midst of a period of unprecedented economic progress, during which black poverty declined, the racial income gap substantially narrowed, black college enrollment mushroomed, and black advancement into the professions took a substantial leap forward. All this, it should be stressed, occurred *prior* to the introduction of government-mandated racial preference.

Hiring-by-the-numbers

Once affirmative action got going, there was no holding it back. The civil-rights movement and those responsible for implementing civil-rights policy simply refused to accept an approach under which preference would be limited to cases of overt discrimination, or applied to a narrow group of crucial institutions, such as urban police departments, where racial integration served a pressing public need. Instead, every precedent was exploited to further the permanent entrenchment of race consciousness.

For example, the Philadelphia Plan, the first preferential policy to enjoy presidential backing (the President being Richard Nixon), was a relatively limited effort calling for racial quotas in the Philadelphia building trades, an industry with a notorious record of racial exclusion. Yet this limited program was seized upon by the EEOC and other agencies as a basis for demanding hiring-by-the-numbers schemes throughout the economy, whether or not prior discrimination could be proved.

Similarly, once a race-conscious doctrine was applied to one institution, it inevitably expanded its reach into other arenas. The Supreme Court's decision in *Griggs v. Duke Power, Inc.*—that employment tests could be found to constitute illegal discrimination if blacks failed at a higher rate than whites—was ostensibly confined to hiring and promotion. But *Griggs* was used to legitimize the burgeoning movement against testing and standards in the educational world as well. Tracking by intellectual ability, special classes for high achievers, selective high schools requiring admissions tests, standardized examinations for university admissions—all were accused of perpetuating historic patterns of bias.

The campaign against testing and merit in turn gave rise to a series of myths about the economy, the schools, the workplace, about America itself. Thus, lowering job standards as a means of hiring enough blacks to fill a quota was justified on the grounds that merit had never figured prominently in the American workplace, that the dominant principles had always been nepotism, backscratching, and conformism. To explain the racial gap in Scholastic Assessment Test scores, the concept of cultural bias was advanced, according to which disparities in results derived from the tests' emphasis on events and ideas alien to urban black children. Another theory claimed that poor black children were not accustomed to speaking standard English and were therefore placed at a disadvantage in a normal classroom environment. It was duly proposed that black children be taught much like immigrant children, with bilingual classes in which both standard English and black English would be utilized. A related theory stated that black children retained a distinct learning style which differed in significant respects from the learning styles of other children. As one educator expressed the theory, any test which stressed "logical, analytical methods of problem-solving" would *ipso facto* be biased against blacks.

Affirmative action begins to crumble

Until quite recently, the very idea of abolishing racial preference was unthinkable; the most realistic ambitions for the critics of race-based social policy went no further than trying to limit—limit, not stop—the apparently relentless spread of racial preferences throughout the economy, the schools and universities, and the political system. Yet it now appears not only that the momentum of racial preference has been halted, but that, at a minimum, a part of the imposing affirmative-action edifice will be dismantled. Furthermore, a process has already been set in motion which could conceivably lead to the virtual elimination of race-based programs.

Racial preferences have become vulnerable mainly because of the sudden collapse of the elite consensus which always sustained affirmative action in the face of popular opposition. Where in the past many Republicans could be counted on to support, or at least tolerate, racial preferences, the new congressional majority seems much more inclined to take a sharply critical look at existing racial policies. Equally important is the erosion of support for preference within the Democratic party. While some newly skeptical Democrats are clearly motivated by worries about reelection, others have welcomed the opportunity to express long-suppressed reservations about policies which they see as having corrupted, divided, and weakened their party.

The revolt against affirmative action has also been heavily influenced by the fact that, as preferential policies have extended throughout the economy, a critical mass of real or perceived victims of reverse discrimination has been reached—white males who have been denied jobs, rejected for promotion, or prevented from attending the college or professional school of their choice because slots were reserved for blacks (or other minorities or women).

There is, no doubt, an inclination on the part of white men to blame affirmative action when they are passed over for jobs or promotions, a tendency which is reinforced by the atmosphere of secrecy surrounding most preference programs. But enough is known about affirmative action in the public sector through information which has come out in the course of litigation to conclude that thousands of whites have indeed been passed over for civil-service jobs and university admissions because of outright quotas for racial minorities. It is also clear that a considerable number of private businesses have been denied government contracts because of minority set-asides.

Lowering job standards as a means of hiring enough blacks to fill a quota was justified on the grounds that merit had never figured prominently in the American workplace.

Another major factor in the change of attitude toward affirmative action is the California Civil Rights Initiative (CCRI), which has already had an incalculable impact. The CCRI was organized by two white, male, and politically moderate professors in the California state-university system. The measure would amend the California constitution to prohibit the state government or any state agency (including the university system) from granting preference on the basis of race, ethnicity, or gender in employment, college admissions, or the awarding of contracts. It would, in other words, effectively ban affirmative-action programs mandated by the state.

Though limited to California, the CCRI is at heart a response to the logical destination of affirmative action everywhere in America: quota systems sustained by the support of elites from both political parties. To be sure, policy by racial classification has grown more pervasive in California than elsewhere in America. White males have been told not to bother applying for positions with the Los Angeles fire department due to the need to fill minority quotas. In San Francisco, Chinese students are denied admission to a selective public high school because of an ethnic cap; for similar reasons, whites, mainly Jews and East European immigrants, are often denied admission to magnet schools in Los Angeles. A de facto quota system effectively denies white males the opportunity to compete for faculty positions at certain state colleges. And, incredibly enough, the state legislature passed a bill calling for ethnic "guidelines" not only for admission to the state-university system but for graduation as well. The bill was vetoed by Governor Pete Wilson; had a Democrat been governor, it would almost certainly have become law.

The true impact of the CCRI can be gauged by the degree of fear it has generated among supporters of affirmative action. So long as the debate could be limited to the courts, the agencies of race regulation, and, when unavoidable, the legislative arena, affirmative action was secure. The mere threat of taking the issue directly to the voters, as the CCRI's sponsors propose to do through the referendum process, has elicited a downright panicky response—itself a clear indication that the advocates of racial preference understand how unpopular their case is, and how weak.

A divisive affair

But a note of caution must be sounded to those who believe that current developments will lead inexorably to the reinstitution of colorblindness as the reigning principle in racial matters. The resilience of affirmative action in the face of widespread popular hostility suggests that even a modest change of course could prove a difficult and highly divisive affair.

There is, to begin with, the fact that affirmative action has been introduced largely by skirting the normal democratic process of debate and legislative action. Affirmative action is by now rooted in literally thousands of presidential directives, court decisions, enforcement-agency guidelines, and regulatory rules. These will not easily be overturned.

There is also the complicating factor of the federal judiciary's central role in overseeing racial policy. Given the emotionally charged character of the racial debate, the critics of racial preference will be tempted to postpone legislative action in the hope that the Supreme Court will resolve the issue once and for all. But while the Court today is less prone to judicial activism than during the Warren and Burger years, and while it may decide to limit the conditions under which a preferential program can be applied, it is unlikely to do away with affirmative action altogether.

The Republicans will face another temptation: to exploit white hostility to racial preference but avoid serious political action to eliminate it. A powerful political logic lies behind this temptation, since getting rid of affirmative action would also deprive the Republicans of a potent wedge issue. Yet one can hardly imagine a less desirable outcome than a prolonged and angry political confrontation over race. Moreover, if responsible politicians who share a principled opposition to preference decline to take the initiative, the door will be opened to racists and unscrupulous demagogues.

An additional obstacle to change is the fact that eliminating affirmative action does not offer much of a financial payoff. Affirmative action is not expensive; its only direct cost to the taxpayer is the expense of maintaining civil-rights agencies like the EEOC.

White males have been told not to bother applying for positions with the Los Angeles fire department due to the need to fill minority quotas.

Claims have been made that affirmative action does represent a major cost to the American economy, but the facts are unclear since neither the media nor scholarly researchers nor the corporations themselves have shown an interest in undertaking an investigation of its economic impact. Indeed, though affirmative action is one of the most intensely discussed social issues of the day, it is probably the least researched. Press coverage is generally limited to the political debate; seldom are stories done about the actual functioning of affirmative-action programs. Nor is there much serious scholarly investigation of such questions as affirmative action's impact on employee morale, the performance of students admitted to college on an affirmative-action track, or the degree to which contract set-asides have contributed to the establishment of stable minority businesses.

Given the truly massive amount of research devoted to racial issues over the years, the lack of attention to preferential policies raises the suspicion that what has been operating here is a deliberate decision to avoid knowing the details of affirmative action's inner workings out of fear of the public reaction.

The diversity principle

Opponents of racial preference must also contend with the widespread acceptance of the "diversity" principle within certain key institutions. Here the American university stands out for its uncritical embrace of the notion that, as one recent cliché has it, "diversity is part of excellence." When Francis Lawrence, the president of Rutgers University, came under fire for uttering the now-famous phrase [in which he referred to African American students as lacking "that genetic, heredity background" needed to score well on college entrance exams] which seemed to question the genetic capabilities of black students, his principal defense—indeed practically his only defense—was that he had increased minority enrollment at Rutgers and during a previous administrative stint at Tulane. True to form, no one bothered to ask how black students recruited under Lawrence's diversity initiatives had fared academically or psychologically, or how the campus racial atmosphere had been affected, or how much standards had been adjusted to achieve the quota. The body count, and the body count alone, was what mattered for Lawrence, and, it would seem, for administrators at many campuses.

The diversity principle is also firmly entrenched throughout government service. Most agencies include a diversity or affirmative-action department, headed by an official with deputy-level status, with intrusive authority to promote staff "balance" and minority participation in contract bidding. So, too, private corporations have accepted affirmative action as part of the price of doing business. Large corporations, in fact, can usually be counted on to oppose anti-quota legislation, preferring the simplicity of hiring by the numbers to the uncertainty of more flexible systems and the increased possibilities of anti-discrimination litigation brought by minorities or by whites claiming reverse bias.

But of course the most serious obstacle to change is black America's strong attachment to affirmative action. Race-conscious policies have had no demonstrable effect at all on the black poor, but they are widely perceived as having played a crucial role in creating the first mass black middle class in American history. The claim here is wildly exaggerated—to repeat, the trend was already well advanced before affirmative action got going. Nevertheless, to many blacks, affirmative action has become not a series of temporary benefits but a basic civil right, almost as fundamental as the right to eat at a restaurant or live in the neighborhood of one's choice, and certainly more important than welfare.

Accordingly, black leaders, who are always quick to condemn even the most modest changes as "turning back the clock" or as a threat to the gains of the civil-rights movement, have now escalated the counterattack in response to the more sweeping recent challenge to affirmative action. When Governor Pete Wilson made some favorable comments about the CCRI, Jesse Jackson compared him to George Wallace [former governor famous for his opposition to desegregation] blocking the schoolhouse door in Jim Crow Alabama. And when congressional Republicans moved to rescind a set-aside program in the communications industry, Representative Charles Rangel, a Democrat from Harlem, declared that the move reflected a Nazi-like mindset.

It is true that many blacks are ambivalent about preferences, or even critical of them. At the same time, however, they are highly sensitive to perceptions of white assaults on civil rights, and they may well find polemics of the Jackson and Rangel variety persuasive.

Eliminating preference programs

Confronted with all these obstacles, some opponents of affirmative action are leaning toward a compromise strategy involving a program-by-program review. This would be a serious mistake; the most desirable and politically effective course would be federal legislation modeled on the CCRI. Such a measure would leave in place the old laws against discrimination but would eliminate all federal programs which extend preference on the basis of race (as well as ethnicity or gender).

The measure could conceivably take the form of a reaffirmation of the sections of the 1964 Civil Rights Act dealing with the workplace, with special emphasis on the clauses explicitly prohibiting reverse discrimination. But whatever the specific shape of the new legislation, absolute clarity would be required on the principal issue: there would be no room for fudging, vagueness, or loopholes on the question of bringing the era of race-conscious social policy to a close. The legislation would therefore also have to include an explicit disavowal of the disparate-impact doctrine, under which the disproportionate representation of the races (or sexes) is often regarded as evidence in itself of discrimination, and which has often led to the imposition of de facto quota systems.

The political struggle over this kind of sweeping legislation would be angry and unpleasant. But eliminating both the practice of racial preference and the controversy surrounding it would set the stage for an ultimate improvement in the racial environment throughout American society. On the other hand, an approach focusing on a program-by-program review of the multitude of preference initiatives in an ephemeral search for compromise only guarantees the permanence both of affirmative action itself and of the affirmative-action controversy.

A less sweeping but nevertheless useful approach would be a presidential decree revoking the executive order issued by President Johnson which opened the way to federally mandated quotas. Though (as we have seen) Johnson did not necessarily intend this to happen, the fact is that his directive became a crucial pillar of the affirmative-action structure. With the stroke of a pen it could be rescinded.

Restoring fixed academic standards

So far as the universities are concerned, the elimination of affirmative action would mean an end to lowering standards in order to fill racial quotas. No doubt this would also mean a smaller number of blacks at the elite universities, but there are perfectly decent state colleges and private institutions for every promising student whose qualifications do not meet the standards of Yale or Stanford. The notion that a degree from one of these institutions consigns the graduate to a second-class career is based on sheer prejudice and myth; for evidence to the contrary, one need look no further than the new Republican congressional delegation, which includes a number of graduates from what would be considered second- or third-tier colleges.

It hardly needs to be added that directing a student to a university for which he is educationally and culturally unprepared benefits neither the student nor the university nor the goal of integration. The results are already clear to see in the sorry state of race relations on campus. Many colleges are dominated by an environment of racial balkanization, with blacks increasingly retreating into segregated dormitories and black student unions, rejecting contacts with white students out of fear of ostracism by other blacks, and then complaining of the loneliness and isolation of campus life. Drop-out rates for those admitted on affirmative-action tracks are high, adding to black student frustration. These problems are invariably exacerbated by college administrators who respond to racial discontent with speech codes, sensitivity training, multicultural seminars, curriculum changes, and other aggressively prosecuted diversity initiatives.

Race-conscious policies have had no demonstrable effect at all on the black poor.

Some have proposed basing affirmative action in university admissions on social class—that is, extending preferences to promising students from impoverished backgrounds, broken homes, and similar circumstances. On a superficial level, this would seem a sensible idea. Blacks would profit because they suffer disproportionately from poverty. Universities would gain from the high motivation of the students selected for the program. And real diversity would be enhanced by the presence of students whose backgrounds differed radically from the middle- and upper-class majority, and whose opinions could not be so predictably categorized along the conformist race (and gender) lines which dominate campus discussion today.

Elimination of affirmative action would mean an end to lowering standards in order to fill racial quotas.

One major caveat is that college administrators, who give every indication of total commitment to the present race-based arrangements, would discover ways to circumvent a program based on color-blind standards. Indeed, they have already done so. Under the terms of the *Bakke* case (1978), which established the guidelines for affirmative action in university admissions, race could be counted as one of several factors, including social class; affirmative action based on race alone, the Supreme Court said, could not pass muster. As matters have evolved, affirmative action on many state campuses, most notably those in California, is based almost exclusively on race and ethnicity.

A similar class-based formula is difficult to envision outside the realm of university admissions. Yet there is no reason to assume that private businesses would respond to the elimination of government-enforced affirmative action by refusing to hire and promote qualified blacks. A return to race-neutral government policies would also enable black executives and professionals to shed the affirmative-action stigma, since no one would suspect that they were in their positions only as the result of pressure by a federal agency. The supporters of preferential policies may dismiss affirmative action's psychological effects on the beneficiaries as unimportant. But the evidence indicates that the image of a black professional class having risen up the career ladder through a special racial track is a source of serious workplace demoralization for members of the black middle class.

Disproportionate numbers

The arguments which have lately been advanced in favor of retaining affirmative action are by and large the same arguments that were made more than twenty years ago, when the intellectual debate over preference began.

Probably the least compelling of these is the contention that the advantages extended by university admissions offices to athletes, the children of alumni, and applicants from certain regions of the country justify extending similar advantages on the basis of race. The answer to this contention is simple: race is different from other criteria. America acknowledged the unique nature of racial discrimination when it enacted the landmark civil-rights laws of the 1960's. Moreover, the suggestion cannot be sustained that outlawing preference based on race while permitting preference based on nonracial standards would leave blacks even farther behind. Blacks, in fact, benefit disproportionately from admissions preferences for athletes or those with talents in music and art. No one objects, or thinks it unusual or wrong for some groups to be overrepresented and others to be underrepresented on the basis of such criteria.

A similar, but even weaker, argument (already alluded to above) holds that America has never functioned as a strict meritocracy, and that white males have maintained their economic dominance through connections, pull, and family. Affirmative action, this theory goes, simply levels the playing field and actually strengthens meritocracy by expanding the pool of talent from which an employer draws. The problem is that those who advance this argument seem to assume that only white males rely on personal relationships or kinship. Yet as we have learned from the experience of immigrants throughout American history, every racial and ethnic group values family and group ties. Korean-American shop-owners enlist their families, Haitian-American taxi fleets hire their friends.

What about the claim that affirmative action has improved the racial climate by hastening the integration of the workplace and classroom? While the integration process has often been painful and disruptive, there is no question that more contact between the races at school and at work has made America a better society. But integration has not always succeeded, and the most signal failures have occurred under conditions of government coercion, whether through busing schemes or the imposition of workplace quotas. In case after case, the source of failed integration can be traced to white resentment over racial preference or the fears of blacks that they will be perceived as having attained their positions through the preferential track.[2]

Government should not be in the business of preferring certain groups over others.

There is, finally, the argument that, since black children suffer disproportionately from poor nutrition, crack-addicted parents, wrenching poverty, and outright discrimination, affirmative action rightly compensates for the burden of being born black in America. Yet affirmative action has been almost entirely irrelevant to these children, who rarely attend college or seek a professional career. The new breed of Republican conservatives may sometimes betray a disturbing ignorance of the history of racial discrimination in America. But on one crucial issue they are most certainly right: the march toward equality begins at birth, with the structure, discipline, and love of a family. The wide array of government-sponsored compensatory programs, including affirmative action, has proved uniformly ineffective in meeting the awesome challenge of inner-city family deterioration.

The end of an era

To advocate a policy of strict race neutrality is not to ignore the persistence of race consciousness, racial fears, racial solidarity, racial envy, or racial prejudice. It is, rather, to declare that government should not be in the business of preferring certain groups over others. Because it got into this business, the United States has been moved dangerously close to a country with an officially sanctioned racial spoils system. Even Justice Blackmun was concerned about this kind of thing. In his *Bakke* opinion, Blackmun made it clear that preferential remedies should be regarded as temporary, and he speculated that race-conscious policies could be eliminated in ten years—that is, by the end of the 1980's.

Affirmative action's supporters grow uncomfortable when reminded of Blackmun's stipulation, which clashes with their secret conviction that preferences will be needed forever. Despite considerable evidence to the contrary, they believe that racism (and sexism) pervade American life, and they can always find a study, a statistic, or an anecdote to justify their prejudice.

If racial preference is not eliminated now, when a powerful national momentum favors resolving the issue once and for all, the result may well be the permanent institutionalization of affirmative action, though probably at a somewhat less expansive level than is the case right now. Alternatively, a cosmetic solution, which eliminates a few minor policies while leaving the foundation of racial preference in place, could trigger a permanent and much more divisive racial debate, with a mushrooming of state referenda on preference and the growing influence of extremists of both races.

It is clear that a bipartisan majority believes that the era of racial preference should be brought to a close. It will take an unusual amount of political determination and courage to act decisively on this belief. But the consequences of a failure to act could haunt American political life for years to come.

Notes

1. Affirmative action has, of course, been extended to women and certain other groups, but I will confine the discussion here to race. Affirmative action was devised primarily to promote the economic status of blacks, and the racial implications of the debate over this policy are far more significant than questions arising from preferences for women or other ethnic minorities. I should add that if preference for black Americans is unjustified, there is even less to be said for it when applied to women or to such immigrant groups as Hispanics and Asians.

2. An important exception is the military, where affirmative action is applied to promotions but where standards have not been lowered to enlarge the pool of qualified black applicants.

8

Class-Based Affirmative Action Is Misguided

Abigail Thernstrom

Abigail Thernstrom teaches at Boston University's School of Education and is a senior fellow at the Manhattan Institute. She serves as a board member for the Center for Equal Opportunity and has written Whose Vote Counts? Affirmative Action and Minority Voting Rights.

Republican opponents of affirmative action are pushing for legislation to end racial- and gender-based preferences. Yet concern about appearing mean-spirited to the voting public has led some of them to endorse a new class-based alternative. Class-based affirmative action, however, is doomed to fail and should be staunchly resisted for several reasons: 1) minorities will lose out to whites who outnumber them among the poor; 2) deciding which factors qualify a person as disadvantaged promises to be problematic and confusing; 3) people will feel encouraged to redefine themselves as victims in increasing numbers; 4) focusing on victimization falsely portrays U.S. society as one of unyielding castes and obscures the real opportunity for social mobility that is the cornerstone of Americans' heritage.

If the rhetoric of mid-1995 is any indication, a staple of the liberal agenda for the past three decades—government programs that give preferences to women and minorities—is in grave danger of extinction.

Threats to affirmative action

On June 1, 1995, California governor Pete Wilson issued an executive order that abolished preferences in state employment for minorities and women, and similar initiatives might follow on the ballots in other states.

In Congress, Senate Majority Leader Bob Dole has questioned the wisdom of affirmative action laws, as has Senator Phil Gramm (R-Tex.). Meanwhile, Florida Representative Charles T. Canady (R) is working on a bill abolishing preferences in federal programs and believes the leadership will go along.

Abigail Thernstrom, "A Class Backwards Idea," *The Washington Post*, June 11, 1995. Reprinted by permission.

84

President Clinton has been in on the act as well. In February of 1995, he announced "an intense, urgent" review of preferential policies, promising a prompt decision. Three months later, his much ballyhooed review turned into a preliminary draft of uncertain status, but the leaked copy is being taken seriously by Representative Kweisi Mfume (D-Md.). In a press conference held the following month, the former chairman of the Congressional Black Caucus warned that Clinton risked losing the support of minority voters by cutting back on affirmative action policies.

Substituting class for race

Mfume may worry excessively. The White House remains stalled in indecision. And while Canady and other Republicans are indeed assembling an anti–affirmative action strategy, they know that, politically, it is wiser to give than to take away. And so, while they appear ready to lock the front door on affirmative action, they may be leaving the back door ajar.

Or at least that is the possibility lurking in Canady's bill. Dubbed the Equal Opportunity Act of 1995, the legislation would prevent the federal government from using race, color, ethnic origin or gender to determine who gets what in the way of federal jobs, contracts and other benefits. But there's a catch: "Where appropriate," Canady said in a letter to colleagues that outlined his bill, "the federal government may still consider the socio-economic status of an individual."

In other words, no more playing favorites based on race, but class may be a different matter. Canady's idea—still in an embryonic state—is obviously not his alone. In early April 1995, for example, the *New Republic* featured on its cover a piece by Richard Kahlenberg arguing for a system that would give preference by class over race. House of Representatives Speaker Newt Gingrich has said he favors re-writing affirmative action laws so they favor the poor instead of certain ethnic groups. Even Clinton, in a press conference the preceding month, said, "I want us to emphasize need-based programs where we can, because they work better and have a bigger impact and generate broader support."

Victim status creep

On its face, class-based policies sound appealing. Why, its growing cast of proponents argue, should the son of a black business executive be given preference over the white child of a trash collector? Why not give a special break to those at the bottom, whatever their race, ethnicity or gender?

But class-based affirmative action sounds better than it is. Any process of sorting individuals into privileged and victim camps rests on a distorted picture of American society—one that sees not social fluidity but rigid castes. Adopting an economic needs test would, more than likely, simply exacerbate the already serious problem of victim status creep.

Once upon a time only blacks got special protection. Today, Hispanics, Asians, Aleutians, Eskimos, women, the disabled and those with limited English proficiency, among others, qualify for a variety of protective programs. Those who argue for preferences targeted at the economically disadvantaged depict a slate wiped clean and a new start, on a revised basis. But much more likely is that new preferences will be piled on top of those we already have.

The reason is this: If a pure class-based system of preferences were put into place and strictly adhered to, blacks would lose out. Why? For one, in terms of sheer numbers, the majority of people with incomes below the poverty line are white. But blacks would also fare worse under a class-based system because whites from disadvantaged backgrounds seem to have been less damaged by their humble origins. In 1994 white students from families with incomes under $10,000 scored only five points below blacks from families with incomes of $70,000 or more on SAT [Scholastic Assessment Test] verbal tests, and were 13 points ahead of them on math SATs. Thus, as the disadvantaged seek out the preferential slots of college entry and other pathways to prosperity, African Americans are likely to lose out. Are the proponents of class-based preferences ready to take the heat when that happens? The answer is surely no.

Class-based affirmative action sounds better than it is.

The greatly expanded list of people entitled to affirmative action status would delight those who want the benevolent hand of government to rearrange the social order. And it would certainly please the diversity industry. In the wake of the Supreme Court's 1989 *Croson* decision holding that minority set-asides could be justified only as a remedy for proven wrongs, numerous cities hired consultants to find the evidence of a racist past that was now required. With class-based preferences, a similar search would likely ensue. Job applicants, municipal contractors and others seeking affirmative action status would employ professionals to spin amazing tales of crippling economic disadvantage.

Playing such games might also profoundly reshape how Americans view themselves. Today, the overwhelming majority of people, when asked by pollsters, identify themselves as middle class; political campaigns based on class warfare predictably crash. But, preferential policies that reward low-income status would encourage citizens to shed their middle-class "illusions" and adopt the language of oppression. The result would surely be a more polarized politics driven by a sense of grievance across the socioeconomic spectrum.

Deciding who qualifies

Beyond these issues of principle is the practical matter of who would qualify as "economically disadvantaged" in a class-based affirmative action system. Who would be viewed as out of the economic loop—injured by economic deprivation? The working class, not the middle class, might be one answer. But the real division in American society is between those who work and those who don't. If only the permanently unemployed were eligible, the program would be small and unpopular.

But if the pool were expanded to include, say, all manual workers, it would become unmanageably large; the skilled auto worker earns more than the white collar bank clerk. Income could be the test, but some people work two jobs while others are employed part-time; would we penalize the former and reward the latter? And whose income would count—that of individuals or that of their entire families? And over what period?

A contractor's work is often seasonal; one year may be better than another. Then there is the question of newly minted college students. Can they qualify for special treatment by demonstrating a meager income from part-time work taken on as they finished their education?

Or perhaps it's not current income but family background that would count. If so, a handicapped mother, an alcoholic father, a depressed sister and a drug-dealing brother would all be pluses, while a two-parent household would be a definite minus. The whole system would certainly make for colorful reading. Applicants to schools and candidates for jobs would be eagerly telling tales of the dreadful dysfunctional families whence they came—the 1992 Democratic National Convention writ large.

But precisely how many extra points would a history of family alcoholism be worth? Presumably, SAT scores would be normed for class status. To what degree? What about typing tests? And when a subcontractor, age 50, submitted a bid to build guard rails on a Colorado highway, would the social status of his parents still be relevant?

An invitation to mischief

Class-based affirmative action, if taken seriously, is one big, feel-good mess. It's a psychological prop for those who need a way of saying, "I care; my heart bleeds too; I feel your pain."

Canady knows this. He has no intention, he says, of leading his troops down such a dangerous path. He simply wants a principled bill that ends discrimination on the basis of race (and other ascribed characteristics) and that is sufficiently modest to be politically possible.

Preferential policies that reward low-income status would encourage citizens to shed their middle-class "illusions" and adopt the language of oppression.

But Canady also knows that Republicans tend to get the jitters when the subject is race. And for those with the shakes, class-based benefits sound good. As one Capitol Hill staffer put it, "They're an inoculation strategy." Their point is to protect Republicans against attacks from those who characterize them as mean. And as such, they have deep appeal across the political spectrum, in fact, which is why the president was briefly on board.

That appeal should be resisted. Class-based preferences, like those being considered as part of the Canady legislation, are an invitation to mischief and won't work. Indeed those who truly care about the less fortunate will embrace quite a different policy—one that delivers the message that, black or white, rich or poor, with effort and discipline the chances are good you can make it. America is a land of opportunity. It's a message of hope, and it's even true.

Organizations to Contact

The editors have compiled the following list of organizations concerned with the issues debated in this book. The descriptions are derived from materials provided by the organizations. All have publications or information available for interested readers. The list was compiled on the date of publication of the present volume; names, addresses, and phone numbers may change. Be aware that many organizations take several weeks or longer to respond to inquiries, so allow as much time as possible.

American Association for Affirmative Action (AAAA)
3905 Vincennes Rd., Suite 304
Indianapolis, IN 46268
(317) 872-7093
e-mail: TMGA99B@prodigy.com

The AAAA is a group of equal opportunity/affirmative action officers concerned with the implementation of affirmative action in employment and in education nationwide. Its publications include the quarterly *American Association for Affirmative Action—Newsletter.*

American Civil Liberties Union (ACLU)
132 W. 43rd St.
New York, NY 10036
(212) 944-9800

The ACLU is a national organization that works to defend Americans' civil rights guaranteed by the U.S. Constitution. It works to establish equality before the law, regardless of race, color, sexual orientation, or national origin. The ACLU publishes and distributes policy statements, pamphlets, and the semiannual newsletter *Civil Liberties Alert.*

Cato Institute
1000 Massachusetts Ave. NW
Washington, DC 20001-5403
(202) 842-0200
fax: (202) 842-3490

The Cato Institute is a libertarian public policy research foundation dedicated to limiting the control of government and protecting individual liberties. It offers numerous publications on public policy issues, including the triannual *Cato Journal*, the bimonthly newsletter *Cato Policy Report*, and the quarterly magazine *Regulation.*

Foundation for Economic Education (FEE)
30 S. Broadway
Irvington-on-Hudson, NY 10533
(914) 591-7230
fax: (914) 591-8910

The foundation publishes information and research in support of capitalism, free trade, and limited government. It occasionally publishes articles about affirmative action in its monthly magazine the *Freeman*.

The Heritage Foundation
214 Massachusetts Ave. NE
Washington, DC 20002
(202) 546-4400

The foundation is a conservative public policy research institute dedicated to free-market principles, individual liberty, and limited government. It opposes affirmative action for women and minorities and believes the private sector, not government, should be relied upon to ease social problems and to improve the status of women and minorities. The foundation publishes the periodic *Backgrounder* and the quarterly *Policy Review* as well as numerous monographs, books, and papers on public policy issues.

National Association for the Advancement of Colored People (NAACP)
4805 Mt. Hope Dr.
Baltimore, MD 21215-3297
(410) 358-8900

The NAACP is the oldest and largest civil rights organization in the United States. Its principal objectives are to achieve equal rights and to eliminate racial prejudice by removing racial discrimination in housing, employment, voting, education, the courts, and business. The NAACP publishes a variety of newsletters, books, and pamphlets as well as the magazine *Crisis*.

Project Equality
6301 Rockhill Rd., Suite 315
Kansas City, MO 64131-1117
(816) 361-9222
fax: (816) 361-8997

Project Equality is a nationwide program that mobilizes the employment and purchasing resources of religious and other organizations to support equal opportunity employers. Project Equality believes that affirmative action programs are necessary to overcome past discrimination against women and people of color. Its publications include the quarterly newsletters *PE Update*, *Action*, and *EEO News*.

Wider Opportunities for Women (WOW)
1325 G St. NW, Lower Level
Washington, DC 20005
(202) 638-3143

WOW works to expand employment opportunities for women by overcoming sex-stereotypic education and training, work segregation, and discrimination in employment practices and wages. In addition to pamphlets and fact sheets, WOW publishes the book *A More Promising Future: Strategies to Improve the Workplace* and the quarterly *Women at Work*.

Bibliography

Books

Herman Belz — *Equality Transformed: A Quarter Century of Affirmative Action*. New Brunswick, NJ: Transaction Publishers, 1991.

Willie L. Brown, Speaker of the California Assembly — *Affirmative Action: A Policy Paper*. Sacramento, 1995.

Anthony Patrick Carnevale and Susan Carol Stone — *The American Mosaic: An In-Depth Report on the Advantage of Diversity in the U.S. Workforce*. New York: McGraw-Hill, 1995.

Bill Clinton — "Remarks by the President on Affirmative Action," Document No. 0784, July 19, 1995. Available from White House Publications, fax: (202) 395-9088.

Carl Cohen — *Naked Racial Preference*. Ann Arbor, MI: Carl Cohen, 1993.

John Edwards — *When Race Counts: The Morality of Racial Preference in Britain and America*. New York: Routledge, 1995.

Gertrude Ezorsky — *Racism and Justice: The Case for Affirmative Action*. Ithaca, NY: Cornell University Press, 1991.

Julio Faundez — *Affirmative Action: International Perspectives*. Geneva, Switzerland: International Labour Office, 1994.

Rose Gilroy and Simon Marvin — *Good Practice in Equal Opportunities*. Brookfield, VT: Avebury, 1993.

Frederick R. Lynch — *Invisible Victims: White Males and the Crisis of Affirmative Action*. Westport, CT: Greenwood Press, 1989.

Nicolaus Mills, ed. — *Debating Affirmative Action: Race, Gender, Ethnicity, and the Politics of Inclusion*. New York: Delta Trade Paperbacks, 1994.

Russell Nieli, ed. — *Racial Preference and Racial Justice: The New Affirmative Action Controversy*. Washington, DC: Ethics and Public Policy Center, 1991.

Steven Yates — *Civil Wrongs: What Went Wrong with Affirmative Action*. San Francisco: Institute for Contemporary Studies, 1994.

Iris Marion Young — *Justice and the Politics of Difference*. Princeton, NJ: Princeton University Press, 1990.

Periodicals

Mark Ahlseen — "The Economics of Affirmative Action," *Conservative Review*, August 1992.

Jeffrey S. Byrne   "Affirmative Action for Lesbians and Gay Men: A Proposal for True Equality of Opportunity and Workforce Diversity," *Yale Law & Policy Review*, vol. 11, 1993.

Linda Chavez   "Just Say Latino," *New Republic*, March 22, 1993.

Ellis Cose   "The Myth of Meritocracy," *Newsweek*, April 3, 1995.

Stanley Crouch   "Someone Ate My Bowl of Privilege," *Los Angeles Times*, June 18, 1995. Available from Reprints Department, Times Mirror Square, Los Angeles, CA 90053.

Economist   "AA: But Some Are More Equal Than Others," April 15, 1995.

Economist   "A Question of Colour," April 15, 1995.

Barry Finger   "Racism and Affirmative Action," *New Politics*, Spring 1995.

Peter Gabel   "Affirmative Action and Racial Harmony," *Tikkun*, May/June 1995.

Linda Greenhouse   "By 5-4, Justices Cast Doubts on U.S. Programs That Give Preferences Based on Race," *New York Times*, June 13, 1995.

Benjamin L. Hooks   "'Self-Help' Just Won't Do It All," *Los Angeles Times*, July 10, 1990.

Jet   "Who Benefits Most from Affirmative Action?" March 20, 1995.

Kenneth Jost   "After Adarand," *ABA Journal*, September 1995.

Mickey Kaus   "Class Is In," *New Republic*, March 27, 1995.

Michael Kinsley   "The Spoils of Victimhood," *New Yorker*, March 27, 1995.

Richard Lacayo   "A New Push for Blind Justice," *Time*, February 20, 1995.

Nicholas Lemann   "Taking Affirmative Action Apart," *New York Times Magazine*, June 11, 1995.

Nelson Lund   "Reforming Affirmative Action in Employment: How to Restore the Law of Equal Treatment," *Heritage Foundation Committee Brief*, August 2, 1995. Available from 214 Massachusetts Ave. NE, Washington, DC 20002.

Carl Mollins   "A White Male Backlash," *Maclean's*, March 20, 1995.

Jeffrey Rosen   "Affirmative Action: A Solution," *New Republic*, May 8, 1995.

Peter Schrag   "So You Want to Be Color-Blind," *American Prospect*, Summer 1995. Available from PO Box 383080, Cambridge, MA 02238.

Benjamin Schwarz   "The Diversity Myth: America's Leading Export," *Atlantic Monthly*, May 1995.

Roger W. Wilkins   "Racism Has Its Privileges," *Nation*, March 27, 1995.

Index

AFDC (Aid to Families with Dependent Children), 9
affirmative action
  benefits all, 10, 18-19
  changing attitudes towards, 75-76
  as class-based
    already in some college systems, 42
    is misguided, 84-87
    is most relevant to equality, 38-47
    was supported by Martin Luther King Jr., 39, 47
    see also social class
  and contracting, 40, 79
  harms black professionals, 48-64, 81
  has not helped poor blacks, 41, 82
  is necessary to fight discrimination, 22-37
    against people of color, 8-13
    against women, 14-19, 68
      con, 66-69
  is warranted by history, 10, 22-27, 34
    con, 59, 71
  opposition to
    is cross-gender/cross-racial, 71
    Republican use of, 38, 77
    resembles anti-Reconstructionism, 26
  origins of, 36
  perceived as civil right, 79
  and quotas, 40, 69, 72, 75, 80
    are not synonymous, 10, 17, 39
  should be eliminated, 70-83
    because it has lowered standards, 75, 80
    because most Americans oppose it, 71, 83
  was not demanded by civil rights movement, 35-36
African Americans, 10-13, 23, 24-26, 36, 44
  can change stereotypes themselves, 58-59, 62
  have unique history among minorities, 42
  leaders, 73, 79
  professional, are harmed by affirmative action, 48-64, 81
Asian Americans, 10, 11, 16, 24, 85
  and college preferences, 42
  and SAT scores, 46

Bell, Derrick, 43
Bell Curve, The (Murray and Herrnstein), 23, 31
Blackmun, Harry, 70, 83
Black Panthers, 35
Braun, Carol Mosely, 24

Canady, Charles T., 84, 85, 87
Carter, Stephen L., 41, 48
Case, Clifford, 73
CCRI (California Civil Rights Initiative), 24, 47, 76, 77, 79
Civil Rights Act (1964), 31, 44, 68, 74
  not intended for racial preference, 73, 79
  prohibited sex discrimination in employment, 15
Civil Rights Act (1991), 44
civil rights movement
  damaged by opposition to affirmative action, 23
  is less popular now, 36-37
  made affirmative action possible, 35-36
Civil War, 22, 25, 26, 54
Clark, Joseph, 73
Clinton, Bill, 24, 38, 39, 47, 85
  administration of, 43, 72
Clinton, Hillary, 72
Coleman, William, 60
"color-blindness," 72, 77, 81
  calls for are rhetorical, 25, 27
  and the Constitution, 28-29, 31
  of Martin Luther King Jr., 47
Congressional Black Caucus, 85
Cornell University, 48, 49, 63
Crouch, Stanley, 52

Dartmouth Review, 26, 27
DeFunis v. Odegaard, 40
Democratic National Convention, 87
Democrats, 23, 24, 38, 76
discrimination, 8, 9, 44
  definition of, has broadened, 74
  history of, 22-23, 24-30, 37
  not eliminated by meritocracy, 31-34
  against people of color, 11-13, 23-24
    see also African Americans
  against white males, 76, 77
  against women, 8, 9, 11-13, 14-19
diversity, 27, 40, 43, 51, 62
  in higher education, 19, 46, 71, 78, 81
  is euphemism for preference, 72
  in U.S. workforce, 10

This book may be kept

FOURTEEN DAYS

A fine will be charged for each day the book is kept overtime.

1/21/03			

GAYLORD 142   PRINTED IN U.S.A.